A COMPARISON OF THE AFRICAN-AMERICAN PRESENCE IN AN EARLIER AND LATER AMERICAN HISTORY TEXTBOOK

Cora Lee Upshur-Ransome

University Press of America,® Inc.
Lanham · New York · Oxford

148696

Copyright © 2000 by
University Press of America,® Inc.
4720 Boston Way
Lanham, Maryland 20706

12 Hid's Copse Rd.
Cumnor Hill, Oxford OX2 9JJ

Library of Congress Cataloging-in-Publication Data

ISBN 0-7618-1837-5 (cloth : alk. paper)

⊖™ The paper used in this publication meets the minimum
requirements of American National Standard for Information
Sciences—Permanence of Paper for Printed Library Materials,
ANSI Z39.48—1984

To my Parents
Milton A. Upshur and Martha E. Harmon Upshur
To my Husband
Mack

Contents

Preface

When I began thinking about the American history textbooks that I was required to read in high school and college, I remembered that there was very little, if any, information concerning the contributions that the African-American had made to the building of America. Initially, I also wanted to include other minorities such as Hispanics, Native Americans and women in this investigation, but as I reflected on the original purpose of this study, my focus shifted back to finding out if a substantial effort had been made to include African-Americans in more recent American history textbooks.

The 1968 edition of *Rise of the American Nation* had limited information about African-Americans and their contributions. The 1982 edition of this same textbook included more information about African Americans. Consequently, the 1968 edition and the 1982 edition of a general American history textbook, *Rise of the American Nation* were analyzed.

This book endeavors to answer the following questions. What were the reasons for the absence of African-Americans in general American history textbooks prior to 1968? What should have been included in general American history textbooks about African-Americans prior to 1968? How can the distortions, omissions, and misrepresentations about the African American found in earlier American history textbooks be pointed out accurately? How do African-American educators, scholars, and historians view African-American history? What was the condition, climate, or mood of society prior to 1968? What were the needs of special groups in society prior to 1968? What was the presence of African-Americans in American history textbooks regarding subjects such as Early Explorations and Settlement, Education, Contributions, and the Old South? What effect did the absence of information about African-Americans in earlier American history textbooks have on the African-American and Americans in general? Are African-Americans being placed in proper perspective in more recent American history textbooks?

Based on the information gained from this study, the following conclusions can be drawn: there was a significant difference in the portrayal of the African American in the 1968 edition and the 1982 edition of the American history textbook *Rise of the American Nation*. The 1968 edition of *Rise of the American Nation* distorted facts about slavery, but the 1982 edition included more information about slavery and its impact on American life. The 1968 edition of *Rise of the American Nation* gave no African-American views about domestic issues. The 1982 edition of this same textbook included several African-American views about domestic issues.

The African American's image changed significantly in one (1) American history textbook, the 1982 edition of *Rise of the American Nation,* in a span of fourteen (14) years. In the 1968 edition of *Rise of the American Nation,* the African-American was portrayed as a Stereotyped bystander who had no history worth mentioning; however, in the 1982 edition of Rise of the American Nation, the African-American was portrayed as a contributor to and a participant in American history.

The scholarly limitations of this book which are judged to be the findings, and the fact that they are based on the investigation of one individual, and the beliefs that a more diverse group of minorities should have been analyzed, might, in reality, be two of its greatest strengths. Moreover, this book will give future scholars another tool to use in their investigation of whether American history textbooks are representing diverse groups of people adequately.

Acknowledgments

I sincerely thank God, my family, especially my husband Mack, my sisters Mildred Green, Dr. Lucille Kornegay, and Doris Upshur for assisting in the research and typing of this book. I would also like to thank my mentor, Dr. Lefteris Lavrakas, for his suggestions and recommendations during the writing of the manuscript. Finally, I wish to thank the faculty and staff of the English and Modern Languages Department at Bowie State University for allowing me to use their computer hardware and software.

Chapter 1

A Comparison of the African-American Presence in an Earlier and Later American History Textbook

Partial American history has been the bill of fare in the nation's schools since the first bell rang[1]. The African American was either written out of United States history or portrayed in the traditional stereotyped images. Authors have asserted that the African American has no history worth mentioning; they have thought it best to exclude what may have been considered controversial material "about the historically insignificant contributions of minorities" (Schwartz, 1996).

Some questions that continually arise concerning the African American's image in American history textbooks are: How can the distortions and omissions found in earlier textbooks be pointed out accurately? Is the African American being placed in the proper perspective in more recent American history textbooks?

It is not only African American historians, teachers, and students who are asking these questions, but also others, who are beginning to realize that they have been partially educated about American history. Whites who have been deprived of an accurate historical picture have little or no perspective for understanding African Americans. The end result has been disastrous in terms of race relations and finding solutions to one (1) of the nation's current dilemmas.

This study of two (2) American history textbooks, printed by the same publisher at different periods of time, compared the differences in the image of the African American.

Definition of the Problem

Authors of American history textbooks are guilty of omitting the African American from American history for long periods of time. According to many authors, the African American disappeared after 1619 and did not reappear until the events leading to the Civil War. When the African American was not omitted altogether, he was usually presented in stereotyped images, as in one (1) college text, *The Growth of the American Republic* (1950). Their view was: As for Sambo, whose wrongs moved abolitionists to wrath and tears, there is some reason to believe that he suffered less than any other class in the South as a result majority of slaves were adequately fed, well cared for, and apparently happy. Although brought to the country by force, the incurable optimistic African American soon became attached to the country and devoted to his "White Folks."

This idealistic view of slavery is not totally accurate, which perhaps is an understatement. Slaves were constantly seeking freedom and if there were those who were devoted to their "White Folks," then perhaps there were those who were not devoted to their "White Folks." Both viewpoints must be revealed, if American history is to be documented accurately. It is frequently asked if there are significant differences between the African American's image in earlier American history textbooks and his image in more recent American history textbooks. This difference is an important consideration and is addressed in this study.

Purpose of the Study

This study was done to analyze an-American's presence as portrayed in an earlier and later edition of a general American history textbook. The same publisher printed these textbooks. This study attempted to reveal the distortions and limitations found in an earlier American history textbooks concerning the African-American's presence, as well as improvements made in his or her presence in a later published American history textbook.

Need for Study

Historians, teachers, students, parents, and other interested persons have found themselves involved in finding out the truth about the African American's image in American history textbooks. It is essential that American history textbooks today contain accurate information about African Americans. It is important for every United States citizen to know that significant contributions made by the African American were not included in early American history textbooks. It is also important to realize that at least one (1) publisher has tried to put the African American in his proper perspective in a later edition of a general American history textbook.

Design of the Study

This study was undertaken to gather information from two (2) general American history textbooks concerning the African-American's image.

Chapter II
Review of the Literature
Introduction

African-American educators across the nation have recently focused their attention on American history textbooks and the African-American presence. Many African-American educators believed that earlier American history textbooks contributed greatly to the African American's feelings of inferiority. The purpose of this chapter was to review information gathered about American history textbooks' image of the African American.

African-American Historians, Educators, and Scholars View African-American Studies and History

Earl Lewis' article, (1995), "To Turn as on a Pivot: Writing African Americans into a History of Overlapping Disaporas" discusses the history of African Americans and how this history went unnoticed by a premier journal, the *American Historical Review* for decades.

The son of a leading post Civil-War black educator and clergyman, Benjamin Brawley received one of the best education's available to men of his time—undergraduate degree from Morehouse College in Atlanta, a graduate degree from Harvard University, and postgraduate training at the University of Chicago—and became a noted author, minister, and professor. By his death in 1939, he had written a dozen books, garnered the respect and admiration of members of the historical profession, and served as one of the first associate editors of the *Journal of Negro History*. Thus, it is all the more surprising that his interpretive history of African Americans went unnoticed by *the American Historical Review*, the profession's premier journal.

Two and a half decades after the appearance of the American Historical Review's inaugural issue, Benjamin Brawley authored *A Social History of the American Negro*, (1921), in which he wrote, "Other races have come . . . but it is upon this on [blacks] that the country's history has turned as on a pivot."

I interpreted Brawley's comment as meaning that blacks were characterized as having no history worth mentioning; however, it is ironical that many historians, including white historians have concluded that blacks may have more history or just as much history as any other race that has come to America. Therefore, it has turned many of the attitudes about the history of African Americans full circle, as on an axis.

Given that most historians found themselves in lock-step with their time, it is not surprising that most charter members of the American Historical Association and its journal believed that blacks were innately inferior to whites. African Americans may have been a part of the nation's history, but they were not the movers and shakers, nor were they perceived as the architects of their own destines. The social inferiority of Blacks was a given for most white historians; it shaped their work and figured in the conclusions they reached. Appropriately, the black historian Carter G. Woodson, founder of the *Journal of Negro History* and Negro History Week, author of numerous books on black life, and among the group of black historians who challenged the prevailing perceptions of the Negro, wrote in a review of author, Ulrich. B. Phillips' history of slavery, (1915), "In just the same way as a writer of the history of New England in describing the fisheries of that section would have little to say about the species figuring conspicuously in that industry, so has the author treated the Negro in his work." Woodson's critique notwithstanding, few who published essays or reviews in the AHR presented a more complete view of black life.

By the late 1960s, historians openly rejected the Elkins now famous Sambo thesis: Masters according to Elkins exerted tremendous control over their slaves. Allegedly stripped of a sustaining culture, deprived of social or psychic space, enslaved Africans supposedly internalized their subordinate status to such a degree that   their   behavior   became infantile.   In its place, a more subtle portrayal of black life appeared. Historians asked how a people could reproduce so completely as Elkins suggested.   Also, even though a number of historians would come to criticize the methodology and bold assertions of the leaders of the slave revolts,   many   teaching   African-American   history   were   forced   to acknowledge for the first time Herbert Apthesker's important 1943 description of slave revolts. How odd it seemed that the same system that produced Sambo could produce leaders of slave revolts such as Nat Turner, Denmark Vesey and Gabriel Prosser. The incongruities forced a reexamination.

By the 1980s, a concerted effort was under way by African American historians to write African Americans into their own histories. Scholars used words such as self-determination, agency, and empowerment to name the variations of those lived experiences. However, as Thomas C. Holt,(1977),cautioned, the time had passed for fanciful portrayals of truly romantic proportions. Hagiographic accounts, or accounts that focused on religion, were common during the first generations of African-

American historiography; however, these accounts ceased as historians shifted from history of reality that even the powerful histories of black self-determination had to be balanced against the limits placed on individual actions.

In acknowledging race's powerful hold on black life and the nation's history, historians have failed to ask an intriguing and important set of interrelated questions such as from what continent were the slaves imported? What were the differences in the cultures of the slaves who were imported from different regions in Africa? How did the slaves imported from the regions of Africa differ from the population of blacks in the West Indies? What was the method by which they and hundreds of others existed as both African American and Afro-West Indian? How do we begin to understand differences within black communities: How do we define and refine the practice of writing African peoples into history of overlapping Diasporas? In researching and discovering answers to these important questions, historians, black and white, will be able to position the African and the African American in their appropriate perspective in general American history textbooks. In June, 1960, when the Third Annual Conference of the American Society of African Culture met in Philadelphia, Jaja Wachulus, at the time, Speaker of the Nigerian House of Assembly and subsequently Minister of Foreign Affairs and Commonwealth Relations, pledged never to turn his back on "blood of my blood and flesh of my flesh." He was talking about African Americans.

Therefore, the misrepresentations in earlier American history textbooks attempted to alienate Africans and African Americans. For example, the 1968 edition of *Rise of the American Nation* does not mention the African cultures and their significance to the beginning of Western civilization. In addition, this edition does not state that blacks were forcefully taken from their homeland, Africa, and brought to America as slaves. However, the efforts of some textbook publishers to separate African history from African-American history failed because both groups realized that their destines were intertwined, and they could make significant progress in rectifying many of the misrepresentations about them in earlier general American history textbooks if they unified their efforts. As in the past, the *American Historical Review* (AHR) would alternate between playing a central and a peripheral role in the evolution of the resulting debates concerning the African American and his or her history. For example, in the beginning, the publishers of the *American Historical Review* played a central role in ignoring the publications of African-American historians about black history. No matter how prominent a black historian, the AHR chose to ignore him and his publications. However, nearly   a decade and a half after the first issue of the AHR, W.E.B. DuBois, one of the country's most learned 5men, became the first African American to have an article published in the AHR. In reference to W.E.B. DuBois, the AHR adopted a peripheral role. I assume, and I have found no documentation to the contrary, that the AHR's publishers allowed DuBois to publish his article to satisfy black historians who were complaining about the exclusion of African-American articles from the AHR. However, the AHR neither supported DuBois nor his points of view. The AHR remained virtually neutral, waiting to determine how white society would receive the writings of an African American in a white publication. The evidence speaks clearly. After the publication of DuBois' article, there wasn't another   African-American article published in the AHR for nearly seventy years The diversity of the African peoples must not only be written accurately in historical journals but also in American history textbooks. In a widely used racially demeaning book, William A. Dunning's *Reconstruction: Political and Economic*, (1907), the student read that Reconstruction was a period 'dominated by a mass of barbarous freedmen." This typical view of historians also appeared in Columbia University's *White Historians View African_Americans* (50) which celebrated John W. Burgess' assertion that "a black skin means membership in a race of men which had never of itself succeeded in subjecting passion to reason; has never, therefore, created any civilization of any kind." Sociologists, politicians, scientists, anthropologists, and others followed the lead of the historians; therefore, the history of the African-American has been misleading and restricted since slavery. White historians, authors of textbooks and other books omitted what they did not want the African American to know about his or her own history and portrayed what they did include in American history textbooks and other books in the worst possible image. In addition to historians portraying Blacks negatively, the language and use of the word Negro as degrading and negative also contributed to the biased history of the African American. The Reverend J.C. Embry of Philadelphia called for the abolition of the use of "Negro" because it indicated color only, was too narrow to include both Africans and their descendants in America, and unlike the designations of the other "great races of men" had no geographical locus: "This title Negro is . . . a device of our enemies, designed to make us contemptible in the eyes of the world. "Throughout the nineteenth and twentieth centuries, Blacks objected to the word because Whites corrupted "Negro" into such derisive and contemptible terms as "Nigger," "Nigra," or "Negress" (a black woman). Stores often advertised "Nigger goods, "and Nigger" appeared so frequently in textbooks that between 1911 and 1938, the *Negro*

Yearbook (1930) annually included a list of protests by blacks against such practices. W.E.B. Dubois (1903) realized that in order to justify Black slavery and the colonialism which followed it, post medieval Europe was forced to create and develop a myth of Black and Colored inferiority, which in turn became a foundation of Europe's modern world.

Consequently, the practice of Europeans identifying anything   Black as negative and derogatory was a method of decreasing the self-esteem of African Americans (Lynch 1652). Furthermore, in denying Blacks assess to their history, Europeans assumed that Blacks would believe they had no history. However it is difficult to deny one race its history without denying all races their history.

Consequently, the practice of Europeans identifying anything Black as negative and derogatory was a method of decreasing the self-esteem of African had   no   history. However, it is difficult to deny one race its history without denying all races their history. How will students who have been taught only European history function in the twenty-first century?   To say that it will be extremely difficult for them is an understatement because the twenty-first is unable to function in a diverse society will be as obsolete as a 1940 T-Model Ford.

In addition to the limitations and distortions of African Americans in many American history textbooks, probably the most unconscionable act of deprivation, bigotry and hatred occurred when the schools in Prince Edward County were closed to avoid integration (1962). The African-American children suffered most, initially, because most of them had no alternative to public education.   On the other hand, in response to President John F. Kennedy's initiative, which provided funds and staff, the Prince Edward Free School Association—forerunner of the National Teacher Corps—was founded.   Not only were these African-American students denied their history in American history textbooks, but also at this juncture in their lives, there were no textbooks to use to learn the misleading history of the African-American.

Therefore, the self-esteem of these young people should have been permanently damaged; however, Dr. Sullivan, Superintendent of the Prince Edward Free School introduced the most advanced educational techniques: upgraded classes, team teaching, flexible scheduling, and extensive use of audiovisual teaching aids.   Moreover, the children were introduced to music, art, and drama.   By the end of the school year, tests confirmed that previously deprived students had in only ten months advanced scholastically an average of two years, and some had advanced as much as three or four years.   However, most importantly, for the forgotten children of Prince Edward County, new hopes had been awakened and undreamed of possibilities opened up (Sullivan 5-6).

President Clinton has stated frequently that we need the contributions of all our citizens to make this country great. We have seen what happens to a great country when it does not utilize the talents of its entire people. Great countries lose their competitive edge in refusing to educate its entire people. In refusing to educate its entire people, a large percentage of the population becomes ineffective because it does not have the skills to contribute to society.

F. A. Lonsway (1966) suggested that culture and philosophy of education were interrelated.. He realized that if African American students were denied to opportunity to understand citation forerunner of the National Teacher Corps--was founded. Not only were these African-American students denied their history in American history textbooks. At this juncture in their lives, there were no textbooks to use to learn the misleading history of the African American their history, then all students had been denied began to ask why the Black man appeared in the curriculum only in the guise of a contemporary social problem, an essentially pathological specimen. The Black man had, so it seemed, no art, no literature, no history. American history textbooks, even the most recent ones do not include significant information about Blacks who fought in the Civil War. The Fifty-fourth regiment came into existence largely because of the zeal of John A. Andrews, war governor of Massachusetts, who led the movement for Negro troops. In 1863, at his request, Andrews received authorization from Secretary of War, Edwin M. Stanton to organize a Colored regiment of volunteers to serve for three years Massachusetts had a very small Colored population from which to recruit. Within the first six weeks, a scant one hundred volunteers had signed up. Andrews anxiously summoned George L. Stearns and persuaded him to head a committee of prominent citizens to superintend the raising of black recruits. In a short time, Stearns' committee collected $5,000; abolitionists and public-spirited Bostonians gladly made subscriptions to the fund. There upon, Stearns advertised widely; a call for enlistment in the Fifty-fourth was published in dozens of newspapers from east to west (Quarles 1940: 25).

Because most of the commissioned officers were white, many of the Negroes, particularly those in Boston, voiced a strong criticism, perhaps keeping a number of young Colored men from volunteering.

Morgan Freeman, one of the African-American actors who starred in the 1993 motion picture, "Glory," and for which Denzel Washington, another African-American actor won an Academy Award for best Supporting Actor stated that he was unaware of the Fifty-fourth regiment until he researched the historical facts in preparation to perform his role more effectively.

William L. Van Deburg (1984) stated that as an alternative to the white-dominated educational process, Black colleges could have provided important process; Black colleges could have provided important Mentoring and cultural support for black students that were not available at predominately white colleges and universities. During the early decades of the century, Black higher education operated under constraints, which inhibited both the ability and the will of educators to campaign for Black studies. Severe financial restraints were further taxed by allocations to remedial programs for graduates of substandard secondary schools. Available funds more often developed traditional courses rather than Black Studies curricula because those were the courses, which defined the word "educated." Furthermore, white benefactors could not conceive of liberal arts curriculum for these schools, which differed significantly from, that offered by northern colleges.

By the 1920s, there were some seventy-nine Black colleges in the United States. Fisk was recognized as the leading liberal arts school, Tuskegee and Hampton were the most prominent industrial institutes, and Howard, the only Black multiversity.

Prompted by rising confidence and consciousness, Afro-American students began to protest the structure of their education (Van Deburg 1980). Though they moved Black colleges toward curriculum changes, the student protests of the 1920s did not trigger a Black Studies revolution.

Some black educators, nonetheless, saw a way of preparing students for life in white America without diminishing their self-esteem. To Howard University's Kelly Miller, (1970), for example, an ideal Black curriculum would "embrace those subjects which lead (1) to discipline, (2) to culture, and (3) to a knowledge of the facts and factors of racial life."

As Black faculty were trained and hired in increasing numbers, Black colleges began to do a better job of acquainting students with their heritage. Carter G. Woodson (1919) offered a course on "The Negro in American History" to juniors and seniors at Howard University in 1919. During the 1921-22 academic year, Fisk introduced a sociology course entitled "Problems of Negro Life" as well as a class in "Negro Music and Composition. Following a ten-week student protest, Black history and literature were added to the curriculum. fifty-eight Black colleges and universities revealed the existence of over one-hundred courses on Black history, literature, and race relations. (Van Deburg 135).

Today, historically Black colleges and universities continue to provide students with accurate knowledge of their heritage and with assistance in eliminating deficiencies in listening, speaking, reading, and writing.

Furthermore, students are taught about the contributions of African Americans in numerous and varied American history and literature courses, such as African-American Literature and Literature of the Caribbean. In addition, many guest lecturers and keynote speakers on the campuses of historically Black colleges and universities are African American. Moreover, many seminars and conferences are held to address the role of Historically black colleges and universities in education. One such conference was held in the nation's capital in 1990. Dr. Samuel L. Myers, former president of Bowie State University and president of the National Conference on Blacks in Higher Education   (NAFEO) and members of the organization met to discuss their role in education as well as to honor their own. Dr. Myers (Essence 1990) said, "We were able to bring together some of the top leadership in Black Higher Education. As a result of this conference, historically Black colleges and universities will focus their efforts on increasing the number of Black males enrolled in college. Furthermore, the students who attend HBCU's are constantly reminded of the contributions of African Americans such as W.E.B. Du Bois,   Booker T. Washington, Thurgood Marshall, Dr. Martin Luther King, Jr., Mary Bethune, Dorothy Height, Malcolm X, Frederick Douglass, Jesse Jackson, Harriet Tubman, Phillis Wheatley, and so on. The historically Black colleges and universities constantly remind the students on whose ancestral shoulders they stand, lest they forget. Uniquely, students at HCBU's learn about the contributions of lesser known African Americans such as Fannie Lou Hammer, Ella Baker, Amy Jacques Garvey and Septima Clark.

Fannie Lou Hammer, a sharecropper who was born in 1917 was founder of the Council of Federated Organizations, which sent out a call for White northern students to invade the state in a "Freedom Summer"--1964. Moreover, she was a founder, organizer, spokesperson and elected representative of the Mississippi Freedom Democratic Party, formed to give disenfranchised Black citizens an organized political voice to fight for representation in the   Democratic   Party. Black students on HBCU's are constantly reminded of the struggle that Blacks endured to obtain basic civil and human rights.

Ella Baker(Internet) devoted her life to progressive causes, linking organizations, generations and history with her own vast store of organizing experience. Part of the history she made happen was the two Southern organizations that together led the modern Civil Rights Movement, the Southern Christian Leadership Conference (SCLC) and the Student Nonviolent Coordinating Committee (SNCC).

Also, Amy Jacques who was born in Jamaica in 1896 began working for Marcus Garvey and Universal Negro Improvement Association

(UNIA) at its Harlem headquarters in 1918 as a secretary and later became an editor of its widely distributed newspaper, *The Negro World.* The concept of African peoples in control of their own lives, lands and resources was considered so dangerous that mere possession of the newspaper was treated as a seditious act in parts of French-held Africa-- punished by death. She married Marcus Garvey in 1922. Unable to secure a publisher, but determined to secure the movement's place in history, Amy Jacques Garvey published the two-volume *The Philosophy and Opinions of Marcus Garvey or Africa for Africans.*

Another woman activist was Septima Clark, who was born in Charleston, South Carolina in 1877. She ran leadership-tutoring workshops that power-fully influenced young people whose names and deeds became legendary: Rosa Parks, Dr. Martin Luther King, Jr., and the college students o the Student Nonviolent Coordinating Committee (SNNC). She chose leadership development as her contribution to the struggle of African Americans. In 1918, she petitioned the Charleston, South Carolina School District to hire Black teachers, and in 1927 was agitating for equitable salaries for them. Thirty years later, the school board got its revenge by promptly dismissing her and withholding her 30- year pension when she refused to conceal her membership in the Nation Association for the Advancement of Colored People (NAACP). However, that happened after she had helped to do the legal and organizational groundwork that resulted in the 1954 Supreme Court decision outlawing separate and unequal schools.

In addition to providing assistance in academics, and increasing students' knowledge about their heritage, historically Black colleges and universities provide mentoring for African American students. Mentoring helps students to remain focused on their goals. Therefore, a mentor helps students to become acclimated to college and campus life. Furthermore, a mentor constantly encourages students to manage their time wisely. A mentor reiterates the importance of time management and how it can contribute to a student's success. A mentor reminds students that they must allocate time for studying, social activities and personal responsibilities to succeed in college. Consequently, a mentor serves as a role model, teacher, friend, cheerleader, parent, and in any other capacity that will assist the students in reaching their goals. The mentoring program helps to provide the nurturing that African American students need to successfully enter the workplace and society.

Even though earlier American history textbooks did not include information about the contributions of African Americans to the moral and physical building of America, recent American history textbooks portray African Americans as contributors to and participants in American society.

The establishment of Black Studies on the campus of San Francisco State College began 1966. It was initiated and led by Blacks. The Negro Student Association changed its name to the Black Student Union (BSU)to indicate a new identity and direction. Moreover., during the fall of the same year, the Union produced a document arguing for and demanding the first Department   of Black Studies. Continuing their thrust, they established a black arts and culture series in the Experimental college which was also created in 1966 and became involved in San Francisco State college's (SFC) tutorial program for the surrounding community. This and other community service activities signaled the social commitment and service Black Studies advocates would place at the center of the academic and social mission of Black Studies (Karenga 21).

Now that the Black Studies program at San Francisco College (SFC) is mentioned as a part of African-American history in more recent American history textbooks, it is necessary to comment on the political and intellectual challenges that face Black Studies programs on college campuses. Black studies was viewed and posed as a part of the overall struggle to rescue and reconstruct black history and humanity and free black minds and labor for Black people's use and benefit.

The political challenge to Black Studies begins with the continuing opposition and lack of support from campus administrations. This takes many forms, including dismantling, subsuming Black Studies under Ethnic Studies, budget cuts, refusals to grant or support department status and other acts negative to the maintenance and development of Black Studies.

In addition to budget cuts and dismantling, Black Studies face the problem of establishing itself as a department. Karenga argued then and remains true that without departmental autonomy, a viable and effective Black Studies enterprise is difficult if not impossible" (Karenga 1980).

Walton (1974:23) observed that it was this administrative crippling through the refusal to build departments and give economic security through tenure-oriented assignments that contributed greatly to the decline in the academic quality and stability of the black Studies program. As he stated:
. . "Unwillingness of the White controlled educational institutions to make any part of a long-term commitment to Black Studies created a situation wherein the academic quality of Black Studies programs was rapidly eroded by the fact of the unstable and temporary nature of the persons responsible Like the for the implementation of the programs."

Like the political challenge, the intellectual challenge is multidimensional and as mentioned above, affects Black Studies' capacity to meet the political challenge. The intellectual challenge begins with the need of Black Studies to define itself, that is, establish in clear terms in a body of critical   literature its academic and social missions.   "The problem of self-definition is undoubtedly the core of the intellectual challenge for its resolution and has implications for all its other aspects. Furthermore, it appears that unless effective self-definition is achieved, the defense and development of Black Studies will remain not only a problem of theory, but also a practical problem as well (Stewart, 1979).

It is the history of humankind in overcoming social and natural opposition that strengthens the individual and pushes him or her further along the road to ever higher levels of life and daring.

The struggle to defend Black Studies offers similar possibilities of development in the academic world. "Black Studies' need to defend itself, is at the same time a demand to develop itself.   Moreover, whatever unsure steps there were in the past, offer a wealth of lessons for the future (Karenga 1980).

As the word Negro was used negatively by white historians in the past, recent American history textbooks have been using the words African American positively.   The Afro centric idea recognizes the influence of African civilizations on ancient Asia, Greece and Rome.   The most definitive spokesperson for Afro centric perspective is Dr. Molefi Kete Asante, professor and chair of African American Studies at Temple University (PA) and author of the *Afro centric Idea* (Temple University Press).

Former National Education Association (NEA) President, Mary Hatwood Futrell says of the term African American, "It has a more positive connotation than simply calling ourselves Black.   African American talks about our culture, our history, as well as our present standing. The term will help give young people a sense of pride, a sense of heritage, and a sense of identity with our past, present and future" (NEA Black Caucus Material).

Black Studies has come full circle since its revitalization in the 60s. The goal of Black Studies was partially achieved; however, the challenges it faces are great.

Unfortunately, earlier American history textbooks did not mention the history of Black Studies in America, but more recent American history textbooks include information of this important phase of African-American history. Joanne Braxton, author and researcher of the works of African-American women asserted that if American history textbooks had included the history of African Americans, they would have included details about the lives of such great Americans as Frances Harper, Ida B. Wells, and Mary Church Terrell.

Frances Harper was perhaps the most popular nineteenth-century Black poet before Paul Laurence Dunbar. Harper saw herself and her race "as a living force, animated and strengthened by self-reliance and self-respect" (Braxton 39).

In addition, the life of Ida B. Wells; mother of the slave narrative would have been an excellent example of a "fiery reformer, feminist and race leader" for African-American students in earlier American history textbooks (Braxton 91). Although Wells de-emphasizes her personal life in order to focus on her public career and achievements in her autobiography, *Crusade for Justice*, it gives the reader enough of a view of her domestic sphere to round out what she presents of herself as a public person.

Moreover, American history textbooks should have included the life and works of Mary Church Terrell. She was born in 1863 into a wealthy African-American family in Memphis, Tennessee. She was educated and well traveled and served on the District of Columbia School Board for eleven years. In 1896, she became the first president of the National Association of Colored Women, a federation of African-American women's clubs. She toured the country speaking out against lynching and for the civil rights of African Americans. She was equally committed to working for the rights of all women, particularly African-American women.

Mary Terrell's speech in 1906 at the Conference of the National Association of Colored women in Washington, D.C. was a deeply moving statement of what African-Americans faced at the turn of the century, as segregation became enshrined in law in the United States. She demanded that women be given equal rights and protection from discrimination as provided by the Constitution. What is revealed about the experience of African-Americans was proof of the gap between America's proclaimed principles and its application with "a fatal drop of African-American blood percolating somewhere through their veins," the African American was reduced to second-class citizenship (Campbell 441).

Consequently, if the minority presence had been included in earlier American history textbooks in the revelation of these historical facts, it would have added the dimension to American history that all other minorities who have contributed to the building of this country would have added. The Black man participated in wars against the French and Indians. They were at the battles of Lexington and Concord, Bunker Hill,, and with Washington at Valley Forge (Stampp 1968). In January;

1863, the Union War Department authorized the creation of "a special corps" comprised of "persons of African descent" - the 54th Massachusetts Volunteer Infantry, commanded by Col. Robert Gould Shaw. Hundreds of free blacks enlisted, including two sons of Frederick Douglass. When the 54th Massachusetts spearheaded the suicidal charge against Fort Wagner on July 18, 1863, the regiment was showered with acclaim, but that defining event was not its only illustrious moment. After the devastating repulse at Fort Wagner let all of the unit's ranking officers dead or wounded, Captain Luis F. Emilio (1844-1918) emerged as the 54th's acting commander. Emilio's A Brave Black Regiment offers an unparalleled, moving, inside view of the entire history of the 54th, from recruitment through disbandment. The revelation that Black men, runaway slaves, served their country valiantly in the Fifty-fourth regiment, even though the people they died to protect mistreated them, gives all African Americans a sense of pride. To have denied Black Americans these historical facts in earlier Americans history textbooks, was to deny all Americans; therefore, depriving an entire generation of its factual history.

Contrary to what the 1968 *Rise of the American Nation* reported, slaves were not content with their plight. They were constantly seeking freedom. Some of the most notable black abolitionists were Frederick Douglass, Harriet Tubman, Henry Garnet, Denmark Vesey, Charles Lenox Redmond, J. Mercer Langston, and William Wells Brown. The religious impulse that guided these early reformers was the belief that slavery was a sin for which God would eventually exact retribution. These men and women escaped slavery and helped others to escape. Harriet Tubman, through here Underground Railroad helped hundreds of slaves to escape to freedom without losing a passenger. Early in his life, Frederick Douglass inquired into the origin and nature of slavery. Since his questions were put to children only a little older and better informed than himself, the youth did not solve his problems easily. As he wrote in 1848: "The very first mental effort that I now remember on my part, was an attempt to solve the mystery, Why am I a slave?" He was told that God had made all things, that Blacks were created to be servants of White masters, and that God was good and knew what was best for all of his creatures. Since these ideas conflicted with his own ideas of goodness, Douglass continued in search for historical cause. By questioning older members of the slave community, he discovered that several could relate in detail the experience of their enslavement in Africa. Armed with this new information, the seven-year old concluded that it was "not color, but crime, not God, but man" who had shaped the origins of black bondage. This sense of Black history, along with a "burning hatred of slavery" motivated and informed his work and that of his Black colleagues in history, fiction, poetry, and drama" (Van Deburg 51).   Frederick Douglass escaped slavery and joined the Abolitionists Society and dedicated his life to helping other slaves escape bondage.

Because earlier American history textbooks distorted the facts about slavery, African Americans were forced to give their version of slave life many times.   Uneasily coexisting with White authored portrayals of southern plantation life was a world of Black histories, novels, poetry and drama.   Black authors recorded different interpretations of slavery than those accepted by White contemporaries.   Indeed their interpretations varied so greatly from White norms that they might best be described as counter-visions of the Black condition under slavery (Van Deburg 50).

Black Americans sought to assemble and preserve their historical tradition in the Pre-Civil War era, despite laws, which discouraged Black literacy.   Within an atmosphere inimical to self-esteem, Black slaves uncovered and shared knowledge of their group history and culture.   In covert classrooms in the field, cabin, and "hush-harbor," bondsmen learned to mitigate the influence of their masters' allegations of Black inferiority.

Members of the antebellum free black   community explored   literary and library societies.   In a nation, which allowed African Americans little access to formal education, these community organizations provided much-needed support and focus for Black self-education efforts.   Groups such as Philadelphia Reading Room Society, Boston's Adelphi Union for the Promotion of Literature and Science, and the Philomathean and Phoenix Societies of New York City developed circulating libraries, conducted surveys, and sponsored lectures on historical, world, and scientific topics (Van De Burg 51-52).

According to Van De Burg (1984), there would be many more such case studies of Afro-American advancement were it not for the pervasive influence of American racism.   Perhaps if black writers such as Frederick Douglass, Booker T. Washington and W.E.B. DuBois failed to delve into the many intricacies of the slavery-racism continuum later probed by the twentieth-century students of the "unthinking decision," they at least prepared their readers for the development of the 1860s.   Though the antebellum era ended in civil war and legally sanctioned racial slavery disappeared, social and legal sanctions thrived.   During the postwar years, Black historians reminded their people and all others who would listen that those historical studies could function as encouragement to self-respect, self-definition, and intellectual freedom.

A more recent American history textbook, the 1982 edition of *Rise of the_American Nation,* provides more accurate information about slavery and its inhumane conditions, instead of the distortion and omission of facts as occurred in earlier American history textbooks.

In an effort to rectify many of the misrepresentations of blacks that had been perpetuated in earlier American history textbooks, many of the school systems, started having increased numbers of Black staff and adopting some biracial and multiethnic textbooks (Schofield 4, 11). However, it would take years for American history textbook companies to correct or include the information about African Americans in American history textbooks. Today, some American history textbooks, as the 1982 American history textbook that I am reviewing will attest, have included significant facts about the African American and other minorities, such as Hispanics, Asian Americans and Native Americans. Educational reform must be for the purpose of preparing all American citizens to lead healthy and productive lives. In many ways, education for nonwhite students in this country is reminiscent of the beginning of the United States Constitution, "We the People" when that was first written, not all of the people--African slaves, American Indians, Asians, Hispanics and women—were given much consideration. Two hundred and nineteen years later, as this country approaches the 21st century, the educational and democratic processes remain in a condition of disarray (The Blue Ribbon Report 1883).

In the nation's capital, Washington, DC, a financial control board has been appointed to oversee the education of the District's children. In addition, a retired general, Julius Becton, has been appointed superintendent of schools. His first priorities are to secure the safety of the students and to eliminate the chronic disciplinary problems. Moreover, Prince George's County, a Maryland suburban county in the Washington metropolitan area has been debating the effectiveness of busing students. Today, that issue has been delayed indefinitely. Therefore, in the Washington metropolitan area, educational decisions have been made that will ultimately affect our children's future.

A society can be measured, as many have said by the manner in which it nurtures its children. Education--the acquisition of knowledge--is the key ingredient for developing and nurturing children, young adults, and society at large (Gill 1991).

Today, children are not being educated adequately because of insufficient funds. Therefore, one can say that the distortions and omissions concerning the presence of the African American in American history textbooks has come full circle because the inadequacy of textbooks in segregated schools was directly attributed to insufficient funds and discrimination; today, the budget cuts in education are attributed to insufficient funds and the partisan agendas of several

Congresspersons.   Consequently, it will be interesting to determine whether President Clinton will support a budget that eliminates major educational and social programs that protect and secure our children' future.

In summary, American history textbooks were criticized for their exclusion of African Americans and their contributions to the building of America.   This exclusion denied African-American students the insight into the history and culture of their people.   Many African-American educators thought that the study of African Americans perpetuated the culture of all Americans.   African American studies may be viewed as not unnatural, but a vastly overdue development in the programs of institution devoted, in at least one (1) dimension, to the exploration of the world around them.

The African American: From Slavery to Freedom to Slavery

In his pamphlet, *The Negro in Modern American History Textbooks*, Sloan (1966) stated the following in examining the 1962 edition of the senior high school textbook, *Our Nation from its Creation:*

The Negro appeared on the second page of this text *in a*   passing reference that except for Negroes and Indians practically all the colonists were of European origin.   The first official reference came, however, in the usual way when the author stated: Another significant event of 1619 (aside from the arrival of single girls and the establishment of the House of Burgesses) was the arrival of a Dutch ship bringing the first Negroes to land in English America . . . For more than 300 pages there was no mention of the Negro.   Then he was reintroduced in a section with the events leading to the Civil War . . . After Reconstruction, except for two (2) brief references to the participation of Negroes in education programs (segregated) as examples of their progress, almost 400 pages of text passed before the Negro was brought back into the history of the United States (6).

Slavery was characterized by systematic brainwashing.   Slaves were taught to hate themselves and to stand in fear of every white man.   Every medium was used to detach them from prior sanctions and to flatten their perceptions and instincts.   In addition, military discipline prevailed on most plantations, which had a chain of command ranging downwards from the plantation owner to the white overseer and the black driver. Slaves were usually marched to and fro from their tasks in military formation and housed and fed in collective settings (Bennett, 148).

Despite the regimentation and brainwashing, despite the whips and guns and chains, the slaves maintained a sense of expectancy and incredible optimism.   Moreover, this expectancy, this leap of the spirit, sustained them in two centuries of struggle against the slave principles.

There were some slaves who succumbed to the assault on their bodies and minds; and even larger numbers, seeing no way out and facing the certainty of death without martyrdom or monuments, mashed their feelings and went through the motion of obeisance.

Though the history of southern bondage reveals that men can   be enslaved under certain conditions, it also show that their love of freedom is hard to crush.

Kenneth Stampp has written, "The subtle expressions of this   spirit, no less than the daring thrusts for liberty, comprise one of the richest gifts the slaves have left to posterity" (Bennett 149-150).

Earlier American history textbooks omitted the facts about the slaves' quest for freedom, and the agonizing days in the life of a slave.

Solomon Northrup, (1853), was born in Essex, New York. His ancestors on his paternal side were slaves in Rhode Island and belonged to the Northrup family. In 1841, Northrup was kidnapped, drugged, beaten, and sold into slavery by James H. Birch in Washington, D.C. and then shipped to New Orleans, Louisiana, where a trader in the Red River Region of Louisiana purchased him.   Eventually, Samuel Bass of Marksville, Louisiana, originally from Canada, with the assistance of Governor Washington Hunt of New York State, secured Northrop's release in 1853, the year his first narrative was published. In his Narrative, *Twelve Years as a Slave*, Northrop, who spent twelve years in slavery in Louisiana, described the day-to-day routine of slave row. "The hands are required to be in the cotton fields as soon as it is light in the morning, and with the exception of ten or fifteen minutes, which is given them at noon to swallow their allowance of cold bacon, they are not permitted to be a moment idle until it is too dark to see, and when the moon is full, they often times labor until the middle of the night. They do not dare to stop even at dinner time, nor return to the quarters however late it be, until the order to halt is given by the driver." However, this, Northrup said, was not the end of the slave's toil. "Each one must then attend to his respective chores. One feeds the mules, another the swine-- another cuts the wood, and so forth . . . Finally, at a late hour; they reach the quarters, sleepy and overcome with the long day's toil. Then a fire must be kindled in the cabin, the corn ground in the small handmill, and supper and dinner for the next day in the field, prepared." The manner of preparing supper, Northrup said was a parable of life of the slave. "When the corn is ground, and the fire is made, the bacon is taken down from the nail on which it hangs, a slice is cut off and thrown upon the coals to broil. The majority of slaves have no knife, much less a fork. They cut their bacon with the axe at the woodpile. The cornmeal is mixed with a little water, placed in the fire, and baked. When it is `done brown,' the ashes are scraped off, and being placed upon a chip, which answers for a table, the tenant of the slave hut is ready to sit down upon the ground to supper. By this time, it is usually midnight. The same fear of punishment with which they approach the ginhouse, possesses them again on lying down to get a snatch of rest. It is the fear of oversleeping in the morning. Such an offense would certainly be attended with no less than twenty lashes. With a prayer that he may be on his feet and wide awake at the sound of the horn, he sinks to his slumbers nightly (Bennett 151-152).

Therefore, it is apparent that the slave's life was no bed of roses; yet, earlier history textbooks failed to include the significant information about the horrific conditions under which this institution called slavery thrived for more than four hundred years.

Many slaves rebelled against their fate, and this fear of rebellion haunted the white slaveholders. Over 250 revolts are recorded in the Unites States, but only a few have been researched and written on at length. By 1750, 40% of the population of South Carolina was enslaved. Even in New York City, where 14% were slaves, the fear of rebellion was ceaseless.

There were enough riots and rebellions to keep those fears alive. In 1739, Cato's conspiracy at the Stovo, South Carolina, and plantation left 44 blacks and 30 Whites dead. In New York, the rumor of a black plot in 1741 led to the conviction of 101 blacks, of whom 18 were hanged and 13 were burned alive.

Even for the Black man or woman who was freed by a slaveholder, life was difficult in the colonies. Free Blacks were "segregated," that is, separated from White society as much as possible. They lived in Black sections of New York, Boston, or Philadelphia. They worshipped separately or in "Black pews in the White-run churches. Black men could not vote, even if they met the property qualifications; nor could blacks testify in court against whites. Thus, the free community of Blacks lived everywhere on the margins of the White-dominated society.

Before any aggregate of plantation slaves could begin to create visible institutions, they would have had to deal with the trauma of capture, enslavement, and transport. Hence the beginnings of what would later develop in "African-American cultures" must date from the very earliest interactions of the newly enslaved men and women on the African continent itself. They were shackled together in the coffles, packed into lard "factory' dungeons, squeezed together between the decks of stinking ships, separated often from kinsmen, tribesmen, or even speakers of the same language, left bewildered about their present and their future, stripped of all prerogatives of status or rank (at least, so far as the masters were concerned), and homogenized by a dehumanizing system that viewed them as faceless (Mint and Price 42-43).

Because earlier American history textbooks failed to acknowledge these facts, we know that even in such wretched circumstances, slaves were not simply passive victims. They developed social bonds during the long middle passage.

Just as the development of new social ties marked the initial enslavement experience, also, new cultural systems were beginning to take shape.

The beginnings of any new African-religion probably occurred from the moment that one person in need received ritual assistance from another who belonged to a different cultural group (Mint and Price 45-46).

Despite all the barriers that the free Blacks faced, they probably remembered, (How could they forget?), the horrific circumstances under which they were captured and brought to this country and reflected on that experience, and they were determined to survive. The free Blacks made important contributions, which were not mentioned in earlier American history textbooks. Benjamin Banneker, a free Black from Maryland, was a noted astronomer, a mathematician, and a surveyor--a man of practical sciences in a society that valued them greatly. Furthermore, Phillis Wheatley, a former Boston slave, became a distinguished poet in her new language. Moreover, Paul Cuffe, a Massachusetts sea captain who became wealthy merchant, financed schools for free blacks and helped them gain positions in the otherwise unfriendly world around them.

Moreover, this author's great-grandfather, a Civil War veteran, farmer, and carpenter, became a role model for the free blacks because he was never a slave. Just as the American history textbook failed to report the horrors of slavery, they also failed to chronicle the lives of free black men and women who were not only surviving but also thriving in specific sections of the country.

In contrast to the unpleasant life of a slave, the life of a free black was enjoyable. One of the special days in the life of my great-grandfather was "Market Day." The account of Market Day was passed down from generation to generation, and this writer was the recipient of this version.

As the dew penetrated the blades of the recently manicured lawn, and the sun prepared to bestow brilliance upon its awaiting audience, the Ruhspu household slowly awoke from a well-deserved repose.

"Good morning, what day is it?" Great-Grandfather prodded.

Everyone yelled in unison, "MARKET DAY!"

Great-grandfather was a medium build, man with straight black hair and a passion for business. He was a role model for his family, and his authoritative position in it was undisputed. As a farmer, carpenter and businessman, he frequently worked a 16-hour day. He had invested well in real estate and owned in excess of 1800 acres of land. He made a trip to the market several times during the year, but this trip was special because more than market value would be paid to the person or persons who produced the best yield.

Everyone was excited, especially about the upcoming trip to the market. David   was a tall and handsome boy now, but he had been very sick when he was younger. He had suffered with rheumatic fever, and he had not been expected to survive, but he did, and now he was an inquisitive, playful, and loyal 14-year-old. He accompanied grandpa to the market quite frequently because grandma insisted that her miracle child be given special privileges.

Dutifully, grandma prepared a scrumptious breakfast that included fresh fruit such as cantaloupe, grapes, and plums; in addition, she prepared scrambled eggs, fried pears, fried apples, fried potatoes with onions, and homemade biscuits that anticipated being saturated with strawberry, peach, or apricot canned preserves.

Everyone ate hardily, especially the older boys Peter and David who were preparing for the trip. Also, the boys looked forward to stopping by the County fairgrounds after they had unloaded the produce.

Employees, family, and friends had harvested the produce. The fields were worked everyday with the exception of Sunday, which was a spiritual, physical, and mental day of rest. When hundreds of workers peppered the fields, it resembled a camp meeting at the Shore African American Methodist Episcopal (A.M.E.) Church. In the center of the fields stood Aunt Sue, a tall, slender, woman with keen features and gray hair, which she tied loosely with the most elegant blue and white scarf whose presence was an enigma when compared to its ordinary companions.. She talked and picked string beans faster than any other worker. To break the monotony, Aunt Sue sang while harvesting crops. "Leaning on the Everlasting Arms", "Since I Laid My Burdens Down," and "Just a Little Talk with Jesus", were a few of her favorite hymns. In her reasoning, singing these hymns made the day pass faster.

On the left of Aunt Sue stood Uncle Jordan, who could compete with Aunt Sue in the singing and talking categories, but not in the picking. He was a lofty, gray-haired man, with a most unique laugh that sounded like the screech of a battered pigeon. Across the path, in another field, hobbled Uncle Kenneth. Ike's demeanor was a source of laughter for most of the workers. He kept everyone snickering about his various mannerisms, from the way in which he buttoned his shirt to the movement of his feet when he danced.   He was the invariable distraction from an otherwise humdrum activity. In front of Uncle Kenneth towered Uncle Zechariah, a proud, serious, and trustworthy worker. He earned the distinction of alerting everyone to the proverbial lunch break.

Lunch break on the grounds of the Ruhspu farm was amazing. First, everyone scrambled from the fields as if they were fleeing the flames of a stubborn fire. Afterwards, they gathered what they had prepared for lunch and anticipated eating what great-grandmother had contributed to the upcoming feast. Grandma had prepared smoked ham, which had been cured in the smoke house, three twenty-five pound turkeys, fried chicken, barbecue ribs, corn bread, collard greens, strings beans, potato salad, sliced tomatoes, sliced cucumbers, macaroni and cheese, candied yams, and a variety of beverages including lemon-aide, kool-aid, iced tea, and soft drinks. A feast of this magnitude was prepared on special occasions, and today, market day, was special. The success of the trip to the market would determine which workers would be rehired for the next harvesting season.

As the feast began, much of the conversation centered on hiring and firing. Anyone who worked for grandpa knew that he was an honest, sincere, and dependable employer. They knew that his decisions were based on several factors including job performance and attitude. The workers also knew that grandpa would pay them a standard wage for their labor.

Travis, one of the older and most loyal workers, reminisced about his first encounter with great-granddaddy. Travis had come to the Shore as a migrant worker from Florida in 1812. He had only been working at the Norman estates three weeks when he was accused of stealing produce to sell. Although Travis was fired, he steadfastly declared his innocence to anyone who would listen. On this particular day at the marketplace, great-granddaddy became aware of Travis' predicament as granddaddy supervised the unloading of his produce and listened to Johnny Boy's story.

"Well," Travis began, " because I was a new worker, I arrived early, around 4:00 a.m. Although many of the other workers were still asleep at the time I arrived, I could not foresee the problems that arriving early would create. First, there was produce missing, but not enough to represent wrongdoing. However, as time passed, the situation became worse. Bushels of produce began to disappear."

The workers listened with expectancy as Travis continued his story. He told of the night he had been accused of stealing 45 bushels of premium produce, including potatoes, tomatoes, and cucumbers, which were among the greatest moneymaking crops of the day.

Unable to control the tears, Travis wept because of the anguish these events had caused him. He had been wrestled down by three of his coworkers, and old man Harmon stood ready to whack him with an iron pipe if he dare move. Travis was taken to the County jail and thrown into a holding cell. He was there five hours before exercising his right to call a lawyer. Because he could not find a lawyer to take his case, the court appointed one.

His day in court was an exciting day in the County. Everyone who could attend attended the trial of Travis Piccot vs. E.L. Norman. No one gave Travis a chance to win the case. However, the court appointed lawyer was shrewd and perceptive. Although the evidence was stacked against Travis, his lawyer felt confident about being able to poke holes in one of the witnesses' story.

All the witnesses for the plaintiff had been excellent, and Travis was extremely nervous about his defense. After the defense presented its case, it was evident that the lawyer had not been able to discredit the witness. Consequently, Travis was found guilty of stealing produce and fired.

After hearing Travis story, and following his "gut" instinct about people, grandpa decided to give Travis an opportunity to proof his trustworthiness as a worker. So, Travis started working for grandpa on July 15, 1812, and 10 years later, grandpa considered him to be one of his most valuable employees.

As the stories and the lunch break ended, everyone returned to the fields for the final picking before the trip to the market. Great-grandfather wanted to take the best produce to the market, so he always inspected the final picking before the trip. The boys finished loading the wagon, and grandpa, Peter and David headed for the marketplace.

The trip was long and eventful. Their first stop was the Smith farm. Great-granddaddy always took the Smiths' produce to the market because their wagon was not big enough to hold it. S.L. Smith had been a farmer in the County for many years. Even though his farm was not as big as great-granddaddy's, his production was sometimes better because he had several children, sixteen to be exact, who helped him harvest crops instead of attending school. Great-grandfather was an advocate of education, and none of his fourteen children was allowed to stay at home from school to harvest crops. Great-granddaddy's and S.L. Smith's produce totaled 5,000 bushels.

The next stop was Longmont 's grocery store. The store was midway between great-grandfather's farm and the marketplace. The boys were tired and hungry, but excited. There were only twenty-five miles left to travel. Longmont had everything in his store from sandwiches and soft drinks to bicycles and galoshes. Mr. Longmont could supply everyone's material needs from the confines of his store. Great-grandfather ordered a chicken dinner, which included macaroni and cheese, green beans, potato salad, collard greens, and apple pie for dessert. All of this food was absorbed with a tall glass of tantalizing, cold, and appropriately tart lemon-aid. The boys ordered the same meal and beverage because they were growing and they could eat almost as much as great-grandfather. The cost of the meals was $6.00. Great-granddaddy paid Mr. Longmont, and they were quickly on the road again.

The final stop before the Marketplace was Victor's blacksmith shop. Great-granddaddy usually stopped at Victor's on his journey to and from the Marketplace. He wanted to examine the horses' shoes, and decide what needed to be done to prepare them for the winter months. Victor was delighted to see great-grandfather because he had known him for many years, and he knew great-grandfather would listen to his homespun tales with an open mind. Ivan was a short, proud, and chatty man, whom the children said had walrus teeth. Because grandpa was likely to spend at least an hour at Victor's blacksmith shop, Ivan could spin one of his extended 'yarns' or truths, depending on one's perspective.

"One day, Victor began, "the day of one of the most important events in the County, the strangest incident occurred." Ivan's vocabulary was extensive because he had accomplished his trade at one of the Black colleges in the South, Hampton University. Because he had attended college, he was recognized as one of the most knowledgeable men in the community.

He told, with great precision, the story of Cast Out, a horse owned by grandpa's obstinate rival, J. Kelly. He said that everyone was getting ready for the big race at the County fair. Great-granddaddy was excited about hearing the gossip on Kelly. "None of the townspeople," Ivan continued, "gave Cast Out a ghost of a chance to win the race because of his extremely solid competition." Among the other well-known thoroughbreds which included Straight Ahead, Bouncing Beauty, Keepsake, Break a Leg, and Long Knight, Cast Out was the least famous.

"Well," Ivan continued, "thirty-five hundred spectators had come to witness this popular harness race, The Weirwood Heap. Everyone was yelling for his or her favorite. As the shot was fired and the race began, the crowd's anticipation swelled. It seemed that a different horse's name vibrated from the mouth of each of the loyal fans in the grandstand."

Great-grandfather was not prepared for what he was about to hear. According to Victor, as the horses circled the track for the final "leg" of the race, the fans predicted the outcome of the ensuing events. However, according to the announcer, Cast Out had won! The president of the fairgrounds had gestured for Kelly to join him on the platform. No! No! No! No! The crowd roared with defiance, signifying that Straight Ahead won! Cast Out, guided by Kelly, had been so far behind that the announcer thought Cast Out had won the race.   Great-granddaddy enjoyed Ivan's amusing story, which was told in Ivan's comical and verbose manner. After enthusiastic laughter, great-granddaddy summoned Peter and David and headed toward the Market.

Grandpa aimed the horses in the direction of the Marketplace. Oh the Marketplace! The aura surrounding that place was difficult to describe. However, grandpa had done an excellent job in describing it to the younger children who were hoping to make that journey in the future.

"The Marketplace," he proudly began, is an exhilarating and fast-paced commercial exchange.   It is the embodiment of business, entertainment, conversation, and good food.   It is the highest rated interchange on the east coast. Other businesses pale when compared to the efficiency and effectiveness with which the marketplace is managed. Its procedure, about which grandpa was unwavering, was flawless.   It was expected that the unloading of the produce would go as smoothly as it had gone in the past.

Great-grandpa guided the horses into the celebrated Marketplace. All of the regulars such as Reed, Summerfield, Watt and Thomas and of course Kelly pulled in behind him.   Everyone was excited about the yield and wanted to know whose crops would bring the highest price.

Great-granddaddy was pleased with his produce. The long hours that his workers had spent in the fields had paid off. However, the decision concerning the price the crops would yield had not been determined.

Grandpa's crops, as expected, brought the highest yield. He was paid $4.00 a bushel for five hundred bushels, which resulted in $12,000 for grandpa and $8,000 for S.L. Smith. Because S.L.'s and great-grandpa's crops were so exceptional, they had been given more than market value for them.

After the crops had been unloaded, everyone was ready to enjoy the excitement of the Marketplace.   The men headed toward Cooley's Restaurant, and the boys got into the wagon with Charlie, who was bound for the County Fair,

Cooley's Restaurant was always crowded with the regulars and the out-of-towners like Grandpa. Market Day was a special day, and because the farmers had received such high prices for their yield,

Cooley was presenting live entertainment along with the incredible food the chefs had prepared for this big event.

The seven-course meal prepared for the out-of-towners was extraordinary. First the chefs brought the appetizers: oysters on the half shell and shrimp cocktail. Next, they brought a salad deserving of a king. Because it was Market Day, Cooley's chefs could select from the best harvest, and that is exactly what they did. They had chosen the biggest and best lettuce, tomatoes, and cucumbers to combine with their other ingredients in making their most extraordinary salad, the Chef's Salad. The ingredients for the homemade dressing included horseradish, mayonnaise, mustard, vinegar, and oil.

The men ate the salad slowly in order to savor every bite. Great-grandfather said that there was something extremely gratifying about eating one's own crops. He compared this moment to the day he received a blue ribbon at the County Fair for having produced a 50lb watermelon, the biggest one that had been grown in the County. Although Great-granddaddy was only fourteen at the time, he remembered that day as if it were yesterday.

To continue, the chefs brought in the next course, the entree, which included four meats: beef brisket, chicken, turkey, and venison. The vegetables were served as a side dish that included a variety of the marketplace produce, such as, broccoli, green beans, collard greens, turnip greens, mustard greens, and kale. The next course consisted of gourmet vegetable dishes such as fried green tomatoes, fried okra, and hollandaise asparagus.

Finally, it was time for dessert. Everyone was preparing for one of the best courses of the meal. It was going to be mouth-watering dessert. To begin, on the table to the right was a smorgasbord of desserts: apple pie, peach pie, Dutch apple, mince meat, sweet potato, pumpkin, custard, and Boston Crème, to name a few. On the table to the left were many different kinds of cakes such as German chocolate, chocolate, lemon, strawberry, marble, and pineapple upside cake. Also, various flavors of homemade ice cream complimented the various kinds of pies and cakes. Strawberry, vanilla, chocolate, praline, butter pecan, and rum were among the assortment.

Finally, various kinds of beverages were placed in containers for the men's sampling. The beverages included tea, original and herbal, lemon-aid, soft drinks, coffee, and of course water.

The men could barely move after the acclaimed seven-course meal. However, they were grateful to Cooley for his hospitality, and, according to Cooley, the day was young, and they had " miles to go, " before they slept.

The entertainment was next. Cooley had engaged the most popular singers in the community, the Up tones. He suggested that grandpa and the other men move into the showroom. While the men were laughing and talking the M.C. approached the stage and asked everyone to be quiet. "Ladies and Gentlemen," he began. "Tonight our live entertainment features one of the leading groups of today, the Up tones." Their gospel recordings, "Shrug's Courage" and "Look to Him," had been major hits for them.

As they were welcomed on the stage by the audience, which was comprised of businessmen who had just unloaded their crops, The Up tones begin their familiar rendition of "Shug's Courage." Great-grandfather was particularly proud of the Up tones because one of them, Shug, was David's girlfriend, and she would be leaving for the fairgrounds after the show.

As the program ended and the men began gathering their possessions for the long trip home, Great-grandfather wondered what the boys were doing at the fairgrounds.

Peter and David were having a great time at the fairgrounds. When they arrived, they purchased tickets for the various rides such as the Ferris wheel and the octopus. As they were leaving the ticket booth, they met several of their friends: Tony, Paul, Alice, Joan, and Sam. They strolled off together to enjoy the day.

First, they stopped at Paul's Place and bought hot dogs, French fries, and soft drinks. After that, they all purchased cotton candy. Now, they were ready to enjoy the rides. They all rode the octopus until they were barely able to move. Then they all rode the Ferris wheel. They were having a wonderful time, and they did not want to leave.

Finally, they all went to the grandstand to watch the race. After the race, they saw Grandpa approaching them to tell them that it was time to leave.

What a day! What a day! What a day! Everybody was excited about the grand time that they had on Market Day. The boys could not wait to get home to tell their brothers and sisters about their adventures.

As the horses made their way down the long, dirt and winding road, the sun took its last breath and the birds bade the day adieu by singing graciously in the peach tree. Masterfully, grandpa steered the wagon to the end of a perfect day.

This was a delightful day in the life of a free black man. However, neither this story nor one similar to it appeared in American history textbooks. This story, which contrasts the slaves' stories, was not a part of the testimony conducted by the Federal Writer's Project.

Some seventy years after the Civil War, the Federals Writer's Project (a New Deal agency) conducted interviews with more than two thousand surviving ex-slaves, most of them over eighty years of age. These interviews illuminated the experiences of freedmen and freedwomen. As with the distortions and omissions about African Americans and their contributions to America, the testimony about slavery was compiled largely by White men and women. Therefore, not only could the reporter's race influence what he or she chose to record, but also his or her unfamiliarity with black speech patterns affected how he or she transmitted the material.

Similarly, many ex-slaves were apprehensive about relating the truth about slavery in the presence of White reporters; however, "Whether they chose to recall bondage with terror, nostalgia, or mixed feelings, their thoughts, concerns, and priorities at the moment they ceased to be slaves emerge with remarkable clarity and seldom conflict significantly with the contemporary historical evidence" (Litwack, Preface).

In addition to ex-slaves' accounts of slavery and its distortions, many facts concerning how destruction and division between the young and the old, the field slaves and the house slaves, the men and women were all carefully orchestrated by Willie Lynch, a name that few African Americans had heard prior to the Million Man March that was held in Washington, D.C., on October 16, 1995. It is not only amazing that this name was omitted from American history textbooks, but also poignant that significant numbers of African Americans were oblivious to the degree that slavery was contrived and masterfully implemented by White slave owners. Willie Lynch came to America from the West Indies to tell white slaveholders how to keep their slaves obedient, subservient, and convinced that slavery was the best possible condition for Black people. To understand why their most trusted slaves turned against them, most masters need not have looked beyond their own households (Litwlack 158). The answer usually lay somewhere in that complex and often ambivalent relationship between a slave and his 'white folks" in the intimacy and dependency which infused those relations and created both mutual affection and unbearable tension in the narrow quarters of the Big House (Litwack 158).

Northern free Negroes could and did speak out against slavery as free persons in an ostensibly free society. Unlike their counterparts in the American South, who lived with a slave society, they could take advantage of the rhetorical commitment of some northern Whites to the ideals of the Declaration of Independence and speak against slavery, often with more vehemence than they could afford to express against their own treatment by northern Whites (Blassingame 1979).

Southern free Negroes desired education passionately. They educated their children largely through their own private efforts, with some support from White philanthropists. Whites regarded black schools as a nuisance and an unsettling influence, but free Negroes believed education offered an opportunity for economic, political, and social advancement for themselves and their children. When Whites established public school systems for their own children, they generally barred free Negroes from attending or even from sharing in the public funds to support their own schools (Berry and Blassingame 40-46).

The stronger free Negroes refused to sink into despair because of discrimination. Instead, they turned inward emphasizing individual reliance, care, pride, and their own humanity.

Writing in Frederick Douglass' paper, the North Star, in 1853, New York's William J. Wilson described the problems facing the self-conscious black: "At present, what we find around us, either in art or literature, is made so to press upon us, that we deprecate, despise, we almost hate ourselves, and all that favors us. Well may we scoff at Black skins and woolly heads, since every model set before us for admiration has pallid face and flaxen head, or emanations thereof" (Ibid 53).

Seeking to counter such feeling, Black intellects frequently discussed the theme of black pride, which was not only omitted from American history textbooks, but also systematically distorted to present an image of a people without a history and without pride in their race. Yet, John S. Rock, a Boston dentist and lawyer, gave a typical exegesis of the time in his 1858 speech, declaring, "I not only love my race, but am pleased with my color. White men may despise, ridicule, slander and abuse us, and make us feel degraded; however, no man shall cause me to turn by back upon my race."

Many Black countries, including Liberia, exhibited pride in themselves; therefore, black people who were given an opportunity for foreign travel increased their pride in being Americans and in being Black.

As foreign travel increased and the knowledge of oppression and slavery increased, many African Americans realized that no other people have been so displaced and so dislocated. The sin was to create a servile, imitative people, who would serve the interests of white people forever. These people would be so disconnected, so dislocated, and so de-centered that they would have become, after constant bombardment by the White society of the ills of Africa and the wonders of the White society, whatever White society wanted them to become" (Asante 119).

The White scientists explained Africans who fought against such situations as having drapetomania, or flight-from-home madness, whenever women wanted to run away from enslavement; or, they said the person who wanted to fight oppression had dysesthesia ethiopiea, or rascality. Africans who did not want to have these terrible diseases were urged to be servile, and to contain anger, and to control the bitterness they felt about slavery (Asante 119).

More recent American history textbooks have attempted to include more of the history of the people who have been systematically oppressed, exploited, devalued and degraded by European civilization: African Americans, Hispanic Americans, Native Americans, Asian American, and American women.

Several groups oppressed minorities, especially the African American, in many ways. The conservative focused on two terrains of oppression: discrimination in the marketplace and judgments made in the minds of people. Although these forms of oppression were not mentioned in American history textbooks, Cornel West, an African American scholar, elaborates on them in his book, *Keeping the Faith*. He states that the "basic claim of the conservative view of African-American oppression is that differential treatment of Black people is motivated by the `tastes' of White employers and/or White workers. Such `tastes,' for instance, aversion to Black people, may indeed be bad and undesirable--that is, it can be shown that such tastes' are based on faulty evidence, unconvincing arguments or irrational impulse" (West 252).

The liberal conceptions of African American oppression unlike the conservative conceptions highlight racist institutional barriers, which result from the "racist tastes" of white employers and workers. Liberals focus on two domains: racist institutional barriers in the marketplace and inhibiting impediments in African-American culture. "Those liberals who stress the former can be dubbed `market liberals'; and those who emphasize the latter, 'culturalist liberals'"(West 255).

In addition to the conservative and liberal views of African-American oppression, there is also the left-liberal view of African-American oppression. The major index of African-American oppression for left-liberals is that black incomes remain slightly less that 60% of White incomes in the USA. The public polices they support to alleviate African-American oppression focus upon full employment, public works programs and certain forms of affirmative action (West 257).

There are several reasons why these explanations were omitted from American history textbooks. To perpetuate the myth that African Americans were inferior to Whites, it was mandatory that this information concerning oppression of African Americans be systematically and methodically omitted or distorted in earlier American history textbooks.

Another view of African-American oppression is the Marxist view which has tragically produced widespread unfreedom in the communist

East; utterly failed to attract the working classes in the capitalist West; primarily served the purposes of anticolonial mythologies in the Third World that mask the butchery of present-day national bourgeoisie in parts of Africa, Asia and Latin America; and is presently overwhelmed by information, communication, and technological revolutions as well as nonclass-based movements like feminism, gay and lesbian rights, ecology, and the various movements among people of color in the First World. These issues are serious and 'must be confronted by anyone who wishes to defend the continuing vitality and utility of the Marxist tradition (West 258).

These various views of oppression help to explain what earlier American history textbooks failed to explore: underlying reasons for the origination and perpetuation of the oppression of the African American.

In order for White society to control Blacks, it had to teach Blacks to hate themselves. This was a component of the White supremacist discourse which associated black being with Black bodies, "as if Blacks have no minds, no intelligence, or only the sum of their visible physicality; therefore, their bodies become a crucial thing" (West 86).

The problems that beset the black underclass, including family stability, and crime, are themselves manifestations of oppression--the historical and ongoing racism of the enemy without--and to that focus on self-help strategies aimed at the behavior of blacks is to treat the symptoms of oppression not its causes. "No people can be genuinely free as long as they look to others for their deliverance" (West 86).

RACE RELATIONS

American race relations according to Loury, (1995), can be divided into three stages: Pre-Industrial, Industrial, and Modern Industrial.

Pre-Industrial may be designated the period of plantation economy and racial-caste oppression. Stage two begins in the last quarter of the nineteenth century and ends at roughly the New Deal era and may be identified as the period of industrial expansion, class conflict, and racial oppression. Finally, stage three is associated with the modern, industrial, post-World War II era, which really began to crystallize during the 1960s and 1970s, and may be characterized as the period of progressive transaction from racial inequalities.

Because American history textbooks failed to include African American history in them, a number of Negro history books were published. Two outstanding examples were George W. Williams' *History of the Negro Race in_America from 1619 to 1880* (1883) and Edward A. Johnson's_*A School History_of the Negro Race in America from 1690 to 1890* (1891). Johnson dedicated his book "to the many thousand colored teachers in our country, pointing to the sin of omission and commission on the part of White authors, most of whom seem to have written exclusively for White children, and studiously left out the many creditable deeds of the Negro." Johnson charged that these history texts implied that Negroes were inferior if they did not say it in so many words (Wesley 109).

William T. Alexander published his *History of the Colored Race in America* in 1887. Then in 1902, W.H. Crogman issued his major work, *Progress of a Race.* Other notable books in the new Negro history movement included *The Afro-American Encyclopedia; Thoughts, Doings, and Saying of the Race;* W. H. Councill's *Lamp of_Wisdom or Race History Illuminated* (1898); C. T. Walker's *Appeal to Caesar_*(1900); W. L. Hunter's *Jesus Christ Had Negro Blood in his_Veins* (1901); Paule Hopkins' *Primer of Facts Pertaining to the African Race* (1905); and Booker T. Washington's *Story of the Negro* (1909).

These books, written about and by Negroes, were written to counteract American history textbooks, which were written exclusively for White children. These books and the Negro's first biographer, William J. Simmons' book, *Men of_Mark: Eminent, Progressive, and Rising* in 1891 "sought to illustrate the Negro's progress and development in this country" (Wesley 109). Meanwhile, John Edward Bruce and Arthur A. Schomburg were forming the Negro Society for Historical Research in Yonkers, New York. Bruce's book, *The Blood Red_Record,* attacked lynching. Schomburg, a scholar of Puerto Rican descent, urged the study of Negro history as a defense against bigotry. He spent his life collecting and assembling Negro historical data.

Many publishers of American history textbooks thought the Negro had no history worth mentioning, but the fact is that the Negro not only has history, but also, it is deeply rooted in American history. Blacks, no less firmly than Whites, believed that history and education were essential to happiness, moral improvement economic success and progress; therefore, blacks, started their own schools to educate their children.

Most Black nonpublic schools fell into one of three categories: entrepreneurial, institutional, or philanthropic. The entrepreneurial schools were those in which instructional and all other costs were defrayed by tuition paid by parents or guardians on a per-pupil basis. In the case of instructional schools, churches or other organizations provided quarters for the school and sometimes guaranteed the salary of the instructor, though tuition was charged and was frequently expected to cover all costs except housing. Philanthropic schools were organized and primarily funded by persons or groups outside the black community (Curry 148-149).

More recent American history textbooks include information about earlier Negro schools and their contributions to the education of Blacks. It is necessary for all students to know, especially African-American students, that free Blacks in urban America did not "passively await an outpouring of   White   benevolence to educate their children. Rather, they sought opportunities for instruction avidly when available and zealously used such social instruments as they possessed to institutionalize their joint efforts. And if existing organizations proved ineffective or insufficient, they established associations--formally or informally for the purpose" (Curry 154).

Toni Morrison, author of *Beloved,* and recipient of the 1995 Pulitzer Prize for Literature, said that Blacks must love themselves not only in the abstract, but they've got to love their big lips, flat nose, skin, hands, all the way down.   The issue of self-regard, self-esteem, and self-respect is reflected in bodily form.

CIVIL RIGHTS

The last twenty years have been rough ones for America. It is as if the country has been on a perpetual roller coaster ride, plunging into war, crime,   attempted   assassination,   WhiteWater,   extreme   poverty, government shut downs, record unemployment, social unrest, space tragedies and successes, and environmental issues.   The plateaus have been few and far between.

Perhaps more than any Central to these years of turbulent social change has been the problem of how to redress the grievous injustices suffered by black Americans.   other institution, schools have been asked to lead the way in remedying the injustices suffered by black Americans.

More recent American history textbooks mention test scores, grades and the response to paper-and-pencil assessments of attitudes, but the textbooks mention very little about the interactive behavior of black and white children in integrated schools (Rist Preface).

Even though the landmark U.S. Supreme Court decision (Brown vs. Board of Education of Topeka, 1954), outlawed segregation in public schools, it produced no short-term, painless, and quick solutions for significantly improving the education of minority and poor children. The poor self-esteem of generation of African- American children can partially be attributed to slavery and its impact on the minds, will, and hope of slaves.   Many African-American children were unable to interact positively with White children because of the fear and anger perpetuated from negative past experiences.

American history textbooks are guilty of the sins of commission and omission about African Americans. American history textbook publishers have included information that should have been excluded from American history textbooks, and excluded information about slavery and its effect on America that should have been included. For example, American students need to be made knowledgeable of how long and hard many slaves fought for freedom. In addition, the information about the servile attitude of slaves included in earlier American history textbooks needs to be corrected.

Carl Rowan, nationally known syndicated columnist, stated, "We blacks are coming to understand that learning is power. He who would be free must first destroy the basic enemy of liberty--ignorance."

I partially agree with Rowan; however, I believe that many Blacks, including those who started schools for free Blacks between 1800 and 1850 knew the importance of education. Consequently, I believe that is it necessary that American history textbooks present the complete history of African Americans from slavery to "constant struggle and eternal vigilance" (Rowan 201).

EARLY EXPLORATIONS AND SETTLEMENT

Separating African-American history from American history has been like separating Japanese-American history, or Mexican-American history from American history. America has been a nation of immigrants, and all of these people, regardless of their continental origin, helped to make American history.

William Raspberry, a columnist for the *Washington Post,* supports this writer's view in advocating that children learn about the contributions of a variety of cultures in American history textbooks.   Children should learn about the ancient cultures of their people, at least so long as it does not substantially   reduce the time available for learning how to cope in present-day America. In addition, American history textbooks should include success stories.   Black Americans who have achieved owe it to black children to tell them how they did it. They need to talk about these magic moments when--and by what means--we learned we were bright and capable and what was necessary to translate that potential into success" (Raspberry 48).

Few, if any contributions of the African American were ever mentioned in early American history textbooks, but the African American did contribute greatly to the building of America.

Blacks accompanied many of the explorers. Scholars contended that Columbus' pilot was Black. Balboa brought thirty (30) Blacks with him. Cortez was accompanied by a Black, who, finding in his rations of rice some grains of wheat, planted them as an experiment and thereby introduced wheat raising in the Western Hemisphere. Blacks participated in the exploration of Guatemala and the conquest of Chile, Peru, and Venezuela. Blacks were with Ayllon in 1526 in his expedition from the Florida peninsula northward and took part in the establishment of the settlement of San Miquel, near what is now Jamestown, Virginia. Blacks accompanied Narvarez on his illfated adventure in 1526 to the Southwestern part of the United States. There Estevencia, a Black, discovered Gibola, "The seven cities" of the Zuni Indians.

When American history textbooks were written, many facts about Blacks were left out. Blacks who came to the American shores in the early seventeenth century were not slaves, but indentured servants. These men could pay back their passage money and be free. However, by 1661, Virginia made all newly arrived Africans and their children slaves, a condition that was perpetuated for longer than two (2) centuries. American history textbooks did not emphasize that the significance of Crispus Attucks' death was not as the first life to be offered in the Revolutionary War, but in the dramatic connection, which it pointed out between the struggles against England and the status of the Black man. Crispus Attuck, a fugitive slave, was willing to resist England, to the point of giving his life. It was a remarkable thing, the colonists reasoned, to have their fight for freedom waged by one who was not as free as they (Stampp 1956).

INVENTORS

Many of the successes of White inventors were directly attributable to the efforts of Black inventors. The President of the United Shoe Machinery Company of Boston, Sidney W. Winslow, maintained that his business success was due to his buying the patent on an invention by a Black man, J. E. Matzeliger. He invented a shoe-lasting machine, which outdated other mechanisms in use. It held the shoe on the lift by a grip, drove nails into place, and delivered the finished shoe in an operation lasting less than a minute.

Even though this invention was not mentioned in earlier American history textbooks, it revolutionized the shoe industry and made the United Shoe Company the largest shoe manufacturer of the day.

In addition to Matzeliger's invention, a pioneer engineer and inventor in Newark, Lewis H. Latimer, worked with both Alexander Graham Bell and Thomas Edison. He assisted Edison in 1878 and joined the General Electric Company engineering staff two years later.

Two other Negro inventors, Elizah McCoy and Granville T. Woods also served American industry. Mccoy patented an automatic lubricating cup for machines in 1872. The drip cup eliminated the need to stop and restart engines in order to lubricate them. His product was so respected that the phrase, "the real Mccoy" was used to question or confirm the genuineness of his and other products. He secured patents in later years for fifty-seven inventions, most of which are in general use in lubricating machinery today. Woods worked mainly with electricity, the telephone and telegraph. He also invented a steam boiler furnace, an amusement apparatus, an incubator and automatic air brakes. He discovered means to transmit telegrams
protect soldiers. His automatic traffic light was sold to General Electric for $40,000.

Other significant inventors were John Parker who invented a screw for tobacco presses in 1884; William Purvis who invented over a dozen inventions for making paper bags; J.A. Burr, who invented the lawn mower in 1899; G. Grant who invented the golf tee in 1899; J. Winters who invented the fire escape ladder in 1878; J. Standard who invented the refrigerator in 1891; and A. Miles who invented the elevator in 1887.

Although these inventors were not mentioned in earlier American history textbooks, the importance of their inventions lies not only in their value to industrial growth, but also in their being a model of achievement under the most severe discrimination of oppression (Karenga 122). Moreover, these inventions attest to the progress Negroes could make as individuals if granted the opportunity.

Earlier American history textbooks failed to mention the importance of the inventions of African America's most distinguished scientist, George Washington Carver. Even though most of his work was done after the major period of industrialization, Carver was a chemist pioneer in the field before it became a recognized science. Determined to free the South from over dependence on cotton, he encouraged farmers to grow peanuts, sweet potatoes and soybeans and developed hundreds of products from them. In his small ill-equipped laboratory of Tuskegee, he made over 300 synthetic products from the peanut, over 100 from the sweet potato and over 75 from the pecan. Some of his synthetic products were adhesive, axle grease, bleach, facial cream, dyes, fuel briquettes, ink, insulating board, linoleum, metal polish mucilage paper, rubbing oils, conditioner, shampoo, shoe polish, shaving cream, synthetic rubber, wood stain, wood filter, buttermilk, cheese, flour, instant coffee, mayonnaise, meal, meat tenderizer, milk flakes, sugar and Worcestershire sauce. Although Henry Ford and Thomas Edison offered Dr. Carver large sums to come their laboratories, he stayed at Tuskegee. He never patented any of his discoveries, refused to profit from them and instead donated them all to humanity (Karenga 123).

CONTRIBUTIONS

Students in public schools should read about African American in American history textbooks who have contributed to the building of American and who have been reduced to performing the menial jobs of society. For example, Joe Louis was one of the greatest boxers in history. He not only brought fame and pride to African Americans, but he also brought fame and pride to all United States citizens. He was lifted up during his best days. Yet, when his boxing days had ended, he was reduced to opening doors at Caesar's Palace in Las Vegas. He was a great man, but before his death, he was trampled upon and looked at as if he were a "thing" (Jackson 1988).

In addition, Jackie Robinson, the first African American to play baseball in the major league was shunned and humiliated by his teammates; yet, he brought fame and fortune to America by his outstanding athletic performances. In addition, Roy Campanella was another great African-American who played baseball in the major league. He did not play second base as Jackie Robinson did, but he was one of the most outstanding catchers to play the game. American history textbooks need to mention the contributions of these great African Americans and reveal the number of years that passed before the Commissioner of baseball created an award in Jackie Robinson's honor.

THE BLACK CHURCH

American history textbooks should mention the significance of the Black church in supporting the efforts of African Americans from slavery to freedom.

The Black church sustained Blacks collectively by giving them a reason to live amid the adversity and oppression. The Black church obviously began as a spiritual sanctuary and community against violent and destructive character of the slave world. Even after slavery, it remained a wall of defense and comfort against racism and its accompanying attacks on Black dignity, relevance and social worth. Secondly, the Black church served as an agency of social reorientation and reconstruction, morality and spirituality in the face of the corrosive effects of slavery (Blassingame, 1979). The Black church became the first institution to preach and practice collective self-reliance. "The earliest rudiments of the economic mutual development came from the Black church. Bishop Richard Allen founder of the African Methodist Episcopal (A.M.E.) Church, and Absalom Jones, the first Black Episcopal priest in the nation, formed the first officially established church" (Jackson 1988).

The Black church has been a sustaining and enduring force in the African American's stride toward freedom since its inception. However, "It was Martin Luther King," Lincoln observes, who made the contemporary church aware of its power to effect change." Furthermore, he revived its tradition of self-conscious, social activism and thus, broke it from the moderate accommodating tendency which was also a part of its history and which it had exhibited since the death of Bishop Henry M. Turner, one of the great moral leaders in the life of the Black church.

American history textbook publishers are obligated to reveal the history of all people, to do less would be to distort and limit the education of all children.

The Black church was not only instrumental in economic development but also in the development of educational institutions. Jesse Jackson alluded to the significance of the Black church in his speech, "The Black Church: Our Spiritual and Prayer Roots." "We talk about the underground railroad. Well, the Black church was the railway station (Jackson 1988). In the 1850s, before the Emancipation Proclamation, Bishop Daniel Alexander Payne founded Wilberforce University, acting under the authority of the A.M.E. Church." Wilber force University in Xenia, Ohio, is the nation's oldest private African-American university. It has a deep commitment to provide academically excellent and relevant higher education, particularly for African-American men and women. This commitment aims at increasing the probabilities of success in college and subsequent careers for all individuals previously excluded from the mainstream American society.

American history textbooks should tell the relevant history of all people who helped make America great. American history textbooks should reveal that Nat Turner was the Reverend Nathaniel Turner. This information is significant because it gives the reader the knowledge concerning the length of time the Black church, its preachers, pastors, and congregations have been involved in the struggle for freedom. When the lynching confrontation occurred in South Carolina challenging Denmark Vesey, another African American who staged a slave revolt, the A.M.E. Church was band from South Carolina for twenty-five years because that Black church was the base of Vesey's activities.

THE CIVIL RIGHTS MOVEMENT

Moreover, the Black church played an active role in the formation of the Civil Rights Movement. Jesse Jackson stated, "When Rosa Parks had a toe ache, she didn't go t a podiatrist--she went to the Black church. When her feet were hurting, she didn't go to the emergency room of the hospital because something deeper than her toe was hurting. Her pride was hurting. Her sense of existence was crushed, and she went to the church"(Jackson 1988).

Even though Dr. Martin Luther King, Jr., was assassinated in 1968, there was very little written about the significance of the Civil Rights Movement in earlier American history textbooks. Detailed background information about the bus boycott and the methods used by the opposition to defeat the Movement prior to

Dr. Martin Luther King, Jr.'s assassination was not mentioned in earlier American history textbooks.

Because the city fathers in Montgomery, Alabama thought the boycotters would ride the bus on the first rainy day, they refused to meet with them to determine what needs needed to be met. The first rainy day came and passed, and the buses remained empty. Consequently, the bus officials and city fathers expressed a willingness to negotiate.

Dr. King and the Negro delegation set forth their proposals in a meeting with the bus officials and city fathers: (1) a guarantee of courteous treatment; (2) passengers to be seated on a first-come first-served basis, and (3) employment of Negro bus drivers on predominantly Negro routes. However, Dr. King and his supporters realized a long-term solution to their proposals would ultimately depend on a change in the law.

During the meeting with the bus officials and city fathers of Montgomery, Alabama, Dr. King stated why they found it necessary to "boycott" the buses. He made it clear that the arrest of Mrs. Rosa Parks was not the cause of the protest, but merely the precipitating factor. Dr.

Martin Luther King, Jr., said, "Our action is the culmination of a series of injustices and indignities that have existed over years" (King 110).

Dr. King continued to cite many instances of discourtesy on the part of the bus drivers and numerous occasions when Negro passengers had had to stand over many empty seats. Dr. King emphasized that the Negroes had shown a great deal of patience, and had attempted to negotiate around the conference table before to no avail.

After his background remarks, Dr. King set forth the three requests and proceeded to explain each proposal in detail.

After Dr. King's remarks and those remarks from the Negro delegation, the commissioner and the attorney for the bus company began to raise questions. They challenged the legality of the seating arrangement that the boycotters were proposing. In addition, they contended that the Negroes were demanding something that would violate the law (King 111).

It soon became clear to Dr. King and the Negro delegation that Crenshaw, the attorney for the bus company, was their most stubborn opponent. He sought to convince the group that there was no way to grant the suggested seating proposed without violating the city ordinance. The more Crenshaw talked, the more he won the city fathers to his position. Emotionally, Dr. King saw the meeting was getting nowhere, and suggested that they bring it to a close. However, the mayor asked a few members of the Negro delegation to stay over to meet with the officials of the bus company in an attempt to come to some settlement. In a smaller group, with the press no longer recording every word, it seemed possible that some progress could at last be made. Soon after the Negro delegation had restated its position, Commissioner Parks said, "I don't see why we can't accept this seating proposal. We can work it within our segregation laws" (King 111-112).

After the opposition failed to negotiate the Negro delegation into a compromise, it turned to subtler means for blocking the protest; namely, to conquer by dividing. False rumors were spread concerning the leaders of the Movement. Their White employers told Negro workers that their leaders were only concerned with making money out of the Movement. Others were told that the Negro leaders rode big cars while they walked.

Not only was there a conscious attempt to raise questions about the integrity of the Negro leaders, and thereby cause their followers to lose faith in them, there was also an attempt to divide the leaders among themselves.

The height of the attempt to conquer by dividing came on Sunday, January 22, when the city commissioners shocked the Negro community by announcing in the local newspaper that they had met with a group of prominent Negro ministers and worked out a settlement. The terms of the so-called "settlement" were: (1) a guarantee of courtesy; (2) a White reserved section at the front of the bus, and a Negro reserved section at the rear, with first-come, first-served obtaining for the unreserved, middle section; (3) special, all-Negro buses during the rush hours.

Actually, except for the first provision, this "settlement" was nothing but a restatement of conditions that had existed prior to the protest. However, the announcement was a calculated design to get the Negroes back on the buses. With the failure of the attempted hoax, the city fathers lost face (King 124-126).

After Dr. King's arrest for being a "so-called" smart Negro, he was jailed; however, his commitment to the struggle for freedom was stronger than ever before (King 131).

In more recent American history textbooks, the background of and opposition to the Civil Rights Movement are mentioned.

If Dr. Martin Luther King, Jr., were alive today, President Clinton said that he would be horrified to see the mess we have made of things; family breakdown, crime and violence in out communities, youth blowing their minds with drugs and blowing away each other with automatic weapons (King A19).

Although King fought to place African-American history in its proper perspective in American history textbooks, if he were alive today, he would be shocked to read some of the negative history about African Americans. He would also be pleased to read some of the great strides African Americans have achieved in their quest for freedom.

In addition to Dr. Martin Luther King's dream, his wife, Coretta Scott King believes that the impact of the Civil Rights Movement, which was not mentioned in earlier American history textbooks, should be placed in its proper perspective in more recent American history textbooks. "The changes wrought by the Civil Rights Movement under Martin's leadership in a relatively short period (less than 13 years have transformed America). As a result of the Montgomery Bus Boycott, the U.S. Supreme Court ordered the desegregation of public transportation. The Civil Rights Act of 1964, passed as a direct result of the successful nonviolent campaign against desegregation in Birmingham and the 1963 March on Washington desegregated restaurants, hotels, parks and other public accommodations. The Voting Rights Act of 1964 passed as a result of the Selma-to-Montgomery March for voting rights, provided much-needed protection of our right to vote without interference and has had a profound influence on the way this nation is governed" (King 56).

Although the Civil Rights Movement gained much-needed social changes for African Americans, the painful process of reassessment which occurred in the middle 60s produced, perhaps, the most definitive aspect and achievement to initiate a theoretical and practical thrust to redefine and restructure society in Black images and interests.

"Even the integrationists wanted Black interests to be recognized and respected. Even they fought for a society which did not penalize Blacks for their color and which would concede to affirmative action to end and compensate for such behavior; however, it was the nationalist tendency which redefined both society and the world in Black images and interests (Karenga 131).

Many assert that all American history should be included in American history textbooks. If the Ku Klux Klan were included in earlier American history textbooks, then the Nation of Islam should have been included.

Elijah Muhammad, Founder of the Nation of Islam, posed Islam as a necessary alternative to Christianity, which he saw as the oppressor's religion. Secondly, he argued that Blacks were chosen people of God, and that God was Black and the devil was White. Muhammad contended that separation of blacks was a divine imperative. Although the Nation had its beginning in the 1930s, it reached its height in the early 60s.

After Muhammad's death in 1975, the Nation of Islam (NOI) underwent a drastic transformation and fragmentation involving severe criticism of Muhammad, rejection of early Muslim belief about Whites, and the introduction of a strong America and Orthodox Islam (Karenga 189)

The success of Louis Farrakhan, National spokesperson for the Nation of Islam after the death of Malcolm X, will depend on three (3) factors: his own leadership capacity; the extent of opposition from other Islamic groups claiming the Messenger's mantle; his success in building a capable and committed cadre; and his ability to relate positively and effectively to the larger Black community (Karenga 191).

Since the "Million Man March" in October of 1995, perhaps many American history textbook publishers will consider reevaluating Farrakhan's status in the larger Black community and America to determine whether his group, the Nation of Islam, should be equated with the Ku Klux Klan.

BLACK HISTORY

Because African-American history was not depicted accurately, if at all, in earlier American history textbooks, and on college campuses, it was important that African Americans promote their own history. Black History, Black Religion, Black Social Organization, Black Politics, Black Economics, Black Creative Production and Black Psychology.

In publishing general American history textbooks, publishers should consider it an obligation to tell the historical truth. Therefore, if people are to be free, they must be made free by the historical truth of all nationalities and races.

It is significant for students to know that people who spoke out against slavery, both Blacks and Whites, were important in chronicling historical periods in the stride toward freedom.

In speaking out against slavery in his speeches and his publication, the *North Star*, one abolitionist, Frederick Douglass, attacked slavery in all its forms and aspects. He advocated, "Universal emancipation, promoted moral and intellectual improvement of the Colored people, and hastened the day of freedom for three million enslaved fellow countrymen" (Huggins 4).

Earlier American history textbooks are guilty of omission because one might believe in reading the 1968 edition of *Rise of the American Nation* that the African American was illiterate; however, one of the greatest orators of the nineteenth century was Frederick Douglass. If it had not been for the eloquent rhetoric of Frederick Douglass, many Whites would not have heard a first-hand account of slavery and its effect put into perspective. Douglass's speeches moved Blacks to struggle for freedom and many Whites, particularly the abolitionists, to put forth a greater effort in assisting Blacks in gaining their freedom.

Douglass declared a new independence. "I shall be under no party or society, but shall advocate the slave's cause in the way which in my judgment will be suited to the advancement of the cause."

Earlier American history textbooks mention very little about William Lloyd Garrison, the White champion of the Antislavery cause and publisher of the *Liberator*. Garrison was one of those people who argued that Blacks should be given all the rights promised to Americans in the Declaration of Independence. "That should happen," said Garrison, "with ever-increasing fury, not gradually, at some vague time in the far distant future, but immediately--NOW!"

When Garrison started his newspaper, the *Liberator*, he left no doubt about his anger that slavery still survived in America. Nor did he intend like those in the American Colonization Society to use soft words or moderate language to achieve his purpose--the end of slavery (Jacobs 81).

More recent American history textbooks mention Lloyd Garrison in context with other abolitionists, and he rates approximately one paragraph in the 1982 edition of *Rise of the American Nation*.

Earlier American history textbooks implied that the African American had no history worth mentioning; yet, African Americans had been dictating and writing first-hand accounts of their lives for almost a century before the first Black American novel appeared in 1853. It is significant that this novel, William Wells Brown's *Clotel*, was subtitled, *A Narrative of Slave Life in the United States* and was authored by a man who had made his initial literary fame as a fugitive slave autobiographer.

Ever since, the history of African American narrative has been informed by a call-and-response relationship between autobiography and its successor, the novel. Not until the modern era would the African American novel begin to match the rhetorical sophistication and social impact of autobiography. The number of important twentieth-century African-American novels that read like or are presented as autobiographies confirms a recent Black critic's contention that "Ours is an extraordinarily self-reflexive tradition" (Andrews 1).

It is sad and criminal that earlier American history textbook publishers failed to include the rich history and tradition of African Americans. If African-American history had been documented in earlier American history textbooks, it would have enriched the history of America.

> Since African-American history was not included in earlier American history textbooks, it was the eighteenth-century slave narrator who first sang into being the "long black song" of the Black American's quest for freedom (Andrews 1).

Since then, the African-American biography has testified to the ceaseless commitment of people of color to realize the promise of their American birthright and to articulate their achievements as individuals and as persons of African decent. Perhaps more than any other literary form in Black American letters, the autobiography has been recognized and celebrated since its inception as a powerful means of addressing and altering sociopolitical as well as cultural realities in the United States. "Nineteenth-century abolitionists sponsored the publication of the narratives of escaped slaves out of a conviction that first-person accounts of those victimized by and yet triumphant over one's slavery would mobilize White readers more profoundly than any other *The African-American Presence in American History Textbook* kind of antislavery discourse" (Andrews 1).

Textbook publishers should have included several of Frederick Douglass' speeches in the 1968 edition of *Rise of the American Nation* as well as the 1982 edition of the same textbook. One of Douglass' most famous speeches *is What to the Slave is the Fourth of July?* Since this speech was not included in earlier editions of American history textbooks,

I have included an excerpt from the Independence Day speech in this book.

" I am not included within the pale of this glorious anniversary. Your high independence only reveals the immeasurable distance between us. The blessings in which you this day rejoice are not enjoyed in common. The rich inheritance of justice, liberty, prosperity and independence, bequeathed by your fathers is shared by you, not by me. The sunlight that brought life and healing to you, has brought stripes and death to me. This Fourth of July is yours, not mine. You may rejoice. I must mourn.

"To drag a man in fetters into the grand illuminated temple of liberty, and call upon him to join you in joyous anthems was inhuman mockery and sacrilegious irony . . .. For the moment it is enough to affirm the equal manhood of the Negro race. Is it not astonishing that, while we are plowing, planting and reaping, using all kinds of mechanical tools, erecting houses, constructing bridges, building ships, working in metals of brass, iron, silver and gold; that while we are reading, writing and ciphering., acting as clerks, merchants and secretaries, having among us lawyers, doctors, ministers, poets, authors, editors, orators and teachers; that while we are living in families as husbands, wives and children, and, above all, confessing and worshipping the Christian's God, and looking hopefully for life and immortality beyond the grave—we are called upon to prove that we are men?. . .

"Oh! Had I the ability, and could I reach the nation's ear, I would today pour out a fiery stream of biting ridicule, blasting reproach, withering sarcasm, and stern rebuke. For it is not light that is needed, but fire. It is not the gentle shower but thunder. We need the storm, the whirlwind, and the earthquake.

"The feeling of the nation must be quickened; the conscience of the nation must be roused; the prosperity of the nation must be startled; the hypocrisy of the nation must be exposed; and its crimes against God must be proclaimed and denounced.

What to the American slave is the Fourth of July? I answer: a day that reveals to him more than all the other days in the year the gross injustice and cruelty to which he is the constant victim.

"To him, your celebration is a sham; your boasted liberty an unholy license; your national greatness, a swelling vanity; your sounds of rejoicing are empty and heartless; your denunciation of tyrants, brass-fronted impudence; your shouts of liberty and equality, hollow mockery.

"Your prayers and hymns, your sermons and thanksgivings, with all your religious parade and solemnity, are to him mere bombast, fraud, deception, impiety, and hypocrisy—a thin veil to cover up crimes that would disgrace a nation of savages" . . .

Printing this speech or excerpts from this speech in American history textbooks would give all children, but especially African-American children, a sense of truth about American history. There have been numerous myths and stereotypes about African Americans, particularly the attitudes of slaves. Therefore, printing Frederick Douglass' speech might help reveal how some of these myths originated and how many of them were perpetuated.

If American history textbook publishers had wanted to put the importance of
African American social activism in its proper perspective, they would certainly have contrasted the similarities between the rhetoric of Frederick Douglass, a nineteenth century orator, and Jesse Jackson, a twentieth century orator. If Douglass' and Jackson's speeches were compared in American history textbooks, it would leave little doubt in a reader's mind that the rhetoric of the two prominent social activists is extremely similar.

An analysis of Douglass' speech "American Prejudice and Southern Religion" and Jackson's speech "Our Spiritual and Prayer Roots" in American history textbooks would highlight some of the more striking stylistic features to determine how they reinforce the total persuasive effort, and possibly influenced social reform.

In comparing speeches given one hundred years apart, one would be amazed to discover that in 1977, Jesse Jackson also addressed many of the social issues addressed by Douglass in his speech in 1841. Although these speeches were given one hundred years apart, both Douglass and Jackson speak of the prejudice and racism that exists in American society.

Frederick Douglass, a U.S. abolitionist, writer, and orator, was born in 1817 in Tuckahoe, near Easton, Maryland, the son of a white man and an African-American slave. After Frederick Douglass escaped slavery, he became committed to freeing his black sisters and brothers; consequently, he joined the Antislavery Movement and began speaking out against slavery and prejudice.

On the evening of November 4, 1841, members of the Plymouth County Anti-Slavery Society together with "New England freemen" and at least one southern gentleman," reassembled at the church in Hingham, Massachusetts, to consider resolutions postponed during their afternoon session. Urging the audience to support a resolution condemning racial prejudice, Edmund Quincy argued that this 'unnatural prejudice"—not implanted by God . . . will not cease while slavery lasts, for men always hate those whom they injure. Quincy then invited Frederick Douglass to relate his knowledge of such prejudice.

In his speech "American Prejudice and southern Religion" Douglass demonstrates his ability to use various stylistic elements, such as ironic contrast, sarcasm, the simile, the anaphora, and the periodic sentence to give his audience a first-hand account of slavery and to persuade them to vote in support of the resolution condemning racial prejudice.

Surprisingly, Frederick Douglass was only twenty-four and a runaway slave when Quincy asked him to speak of his experiences of slavery before the Anti-Slavery Society. However, many people in the mixed audience, including Lloyd Garrison, President of the Anti-Slavery Society knew that Douglass would be an effective orator against the horrors and injustices of slavery.

Douglass' use of ironic contrast in the opening paragraphs of his speech evoked sympathy for the treatment of blacks; at the same time, he reveals the hypocrisy of the white Christian.

"But among those who experienced religion at this time was a colored girl; she was baptized in the same water with the rest; so she thought she might sit at the Lord's table and partake of the same sacramental elements with the others; the deacon handed round the cup, and when he came to the colored girl, he could not pass her, for there was the minister looking right at him, and since he was a kind of an abolitionist, the deacon   rather afraid of giving him offense, he handed the girl the cup, and she tasted; now it so happened that next to her sat a young lady who had been converted at the same time, baptized in the same water, and put her hope in the same blessed Savior; yet when the cup containing the precious blood which had been shed for all, came to her, she rose in disdain and walked out of the church."

Douglass demonstrates the use of religion by the white Christian as a justification of oppression.

Douglass' application of sarcasm in this example emphasizes the humor, yet the underlying seriousness of prejudice. Douglass' use of sarcasm at this point in his speech appeals to the audience's emotions. In revealing racial prejudice in the church, he gives the audience a better understanding of the extent of racial prejudice and its effects; therefore, increasing the probability of the audience voting in support of the resolution condemning racial prejudice. In addition, these examples will increase Douglass' credibility because the audience will assume that he does not have the time to recount all of his slavery experiences; therefore, his examples are carefully chosen ones from a much larger store of information.

Douglass' comparison of the kingdom of heaven to a net or the use of the simile in paragraph four (4) gives the audience the creation of a sense of how both black and white fish were caught in the same net, yet when the net was brought ashore, the black fish were separated from the white fish. Similarly, both black and white Christians were converted and received the kingdom of God, yet when the white Christian was asked to practice her religion, she was unable to drink from the same cup as her black Christian sister.

Douglass' application of the simile is effective because he compares the discriminatory practices in fishing, an activity with which most people are familiar, to the discriminatory practices in the church. Thus he alerts his audience to how deeply racial prejudice is rooted in this country.

Douglass' application of the periodic sentence achieves emphasis in the first example by beginning with a dependent element and ending with the main thought. "But among those who experienced religion at the same time was a colored girl . . .." He tells his audience that the colored girl sits at the Lord's Table and partakes of the same sacramental elements with the others. Finally, Douglass states that a white young lady rose in disdain and walked out of the church because her colored Christian sister had tasted from the same cup.

Many scholars credit Douglass' eloquent oration in helping to change the minds of significant numbers of people concerning slavery. Douglass was probably the most effective speaker for African Americans I in the nineteenth century.

Similarly, Jesse Louis Jackson, born October 8, 1941, 1941 in Greenville, South Carolina, and one of the disciples of Martin Luther King, Jr. Is one of the most effective speakers for African Americans in the twentieth century. He is credited, as much as anyone, with keeping the Civil Rights Movement before the public after the death of Dr. Martin Luther King, Jr.

Jackson was speaking to a black audience when he delivered his speech "Our Spiritual and Prayer Roots" on February 26, 1977. For nearly two decades, Operation PUSH (and it predecessor, the Southern Christian Leadership Conference's Operation Breadbasket) has sponsored a weekly Saturday Morning Community Forum in its 2000-seat auditorium at its national headquarters in Chicago. National and international religious, political, and business leaders address issues of local, state, and national concern.

Unlike Douglass, Jackson was thirty-five when he delivered this speech. One may say that thirty-five is young, and it is. However,

Jackson had been involved in political activism for approximately fifteen (15) years prior to delivering this speech.

In his speech "Our Spiritual and Prayer Roots," Jackson reminds his audience in his use of ironic contrast, parallel structure, the anaphora, and comparison and contrast to return to their roots, the black church.

Unlike Douglass, Jackson's application of ironic contrast in the fourth paragraph demonstrates to his audience that through all the obstacles, particularly racism and prejudice, Christianity, our spiritual and prayer roots, has been a source of overcoming oppression; rather than, according to Douglass, a source of oppression.

Jackson uses the metaphor as effectively as Douglass uses the simile. "The church has been our rock in a weary place."; "The church has been our foundation in ages past."

Unlike Douglass' opening paragraphs, Jackson chooses allusion rather than example in his opening paragraphs to emphasize the sustaining power of the black church.   In contrast to Douglass' humorous, but serious examples, Jackson alludes to great African Americans, such as Adam Clayton Powell, Shirley Chisholm, Barbara Jordan, George Johnson, Madam C.J.   Walker, Miordecai Johnson, Oscar Peterson, and Ralph Metcalfe, who are the fruits of our labor, but Jackson is interested in the roots of our labor, the black church.

When Jackson alludes to these great African Americans, the audience assumes that he has only named a few of them; therefore, these allusions give him credibility and allow the audience to believe that Jackson is aware of the accomplishments of numerous African Americans.

While Jackson's allusions are of great African Americans, Douglass' allusions are of "no name" hypocritical white Christians, such as women, priests and ministers.

Jackson's use of the anaphora or the repetition of key phrases creates the sense of the urgency in his message. He emotionally asks his audience to return to its spiritual and prayer roots, the black church. He repeats the words fruits and roots and states that the fruits of our tradition lie in the roots of our tradition. In addition, he repeats the phrases "The black church, "Return to our roots, and "Wilt not Thou revive us again?"

Furthermore, I suggest Jackson chose the words fruits and roots to symbolically or metonymically represent progress or success and base or support.   Jackson uses this persuasive device in the opening paragraphs to inform his audience that one can readily enjoy the end result, the fruits; however, it is more difficult for one to remember the sacrifice and labor that produced those fruits, the black church, our spiritual and prayer roots.

Although Douglass and Jackson use different stylistic elements in their speeches, each of them supports his theme, the deprivation and inequality of blacks because of slavery and prejudice and the sustaining force for blacks, the black church, effectively.

In his Antislavery speeches, particularly his passionate speeches against the hypocrisy of Southern and Northern religious leaders, Douglass uses his eloquent oratorical skills to enlighten the blacks and the whites about the horrible effects of slavery; consequently, he influence significant numbers of people to view slavery differently.

Similarly, Jesse Jackson, an advocate for civil and human rights uses his oratorical gifts to influence people, especially black people, to consider their past, and significant the black church was, and still is, in the struggle for civil rights. He reminds his audience on whose shoulders they stand and why it is important to keep hope alive and stride, as Frederick Douglass, toward freedom.

Although these speeches were given one hundred years apart, the significance of their effect is uncanny. Douglass is emotionally appealing to his audience by testimony and circumstance in "American Prejudice and Southern Religion." He tells the audience that slavery is wrong and emancipation is the answer to the ills that plague the land. Similarly, Jackson in "Our Spiritual and Prayer Roots appeal to his audience's sense of pride and obligation in telling them that the fight for freedom must continue. He emotionally explains that if our ancestors survived slavery and prejudice through prayer and other traditions of the black church, then we can certainly survive.

Each orator argues his thesis admirable and differently; however, the goal of the speeches is essentially the same: to assist blacks in gaining the basic freedoms of life, liberty, and the pursuit of happiness that should be afforded to everyone. Even thought these speeches were give one hundred years apart, they both reveal the significance of black oratory in an effort to free blacks from the bondage of slavery, prejudice, and racism.

If American history textbooks had accurately portrayed the African American and his or her contributions, certainly Jesse Jackson and Frederick Douglass would have been profiled or discussed together because their contributions were significant in initiating social reform in society.

Although their speeches were delivered one-hundred years apart, their messages are basically the same—freedom from oppression for the African American. Therefore, all children, especially African-American children, should be aware of Frederick Douglass' and Jess Jackson's impact on society through their oratorical gifts and humanitarian gifts and their vision for America. Both Douglass and Jackson were confident that the greatness of American lay in its ability to utilize the talent of all of its citizens. They realized, even though their speeches were given one-hundred years apart, that there is strength in diversity, and that the African-American's talent would contribute to America's capacity to compete in a global society and to retain its position as the most powerful country in the free world.

Because earlier American history textbooks omitted or distorted African-American history, autobiographers such as W.E.B. Du Bois and Richard Wright sought to repossess their social and historical identities, or dramatize by fictional techniques, the truth of their recreated lives. As both history and literature, autobiography has served the expressive aims of many diverse talents.

"The result is a cultural achievement vastly extending and enriching the tradition Du Bois and Wright themselves inherited from Langston Hughes, Ida Wells Barnett, James Weldon Johnson, Booker T. Washington, and the nineteenth-century" (Stone 171-72).

More recent American history textbooks have mentioned African-American autobiographers such as James Baldwin and Maya Angelou; however, there are several great African-American autobiographers that are still not included in American history textbooks. Because Black autobiography is a powerful force in and a characteristic form of contemporary culture, it is critical that it be included as an important component of American history textbooks.

Today, one hundred years after the death of Frederick Douglass, his slave narrative, *Narrative of the Life of Frederick Douglass*, is readily accessible to high school students. Contrary to earlier American history textbooks, more recent American history textbooks, particularly, the 1982 edition of *Rise of the American Nation*, include a page on the life and works of Frederick Douglass.

Frederick Douglass not only provides students with an understanding of the horrors of slavery, but also helps student understand how they can overcome adversity. Although a slave, Douglass's mind was not enslaved. Douglass's life serves as an example to all children, particularly African-American children. Douglass was denied any formal education and deprived of books and paper, writes eloquently about the importance of knowledge. He also writes "learning is the pathway from slavery to freedom" (49). Perhaps, it takes someone who was denied the right to learn to teach today's students the importance of the education they take for granted. Therefore, it is important that American history textbooks include the historical information about men such as Frederick Douglass who have helped make America a great country.

Contrary to what was reported in earlier American history textbooks, Blacks were no better able to work in the rice swamps and cotton fields than the free White man. However, the Black slaves, unlike the free Whites, could be forced to toil in the rice swamps regardless of the effect upon their health (Franklin 1947).

Contrary to what was written in earlier American history textbooks, many Blacks did not adapt to slavery without a fight. Almost every voyage of a slave ship was a nightmare for the White crewmen. There were hundreds of valid accounts of Black revolts both aboard slave ships and in the cotton fields. Many blacks chose to die as a result of man-eating sharks in the turbulent waters than face enslavement in an alien land (Franklin 1947).

It was not only the mistreated slave who sought freedom, but also the slaves of masters who were not so harsh. As Frederick Douglass, (1855), stated:

Beat and cuff your slave, keep him hungry and spiritless, and he will follow the chain of his master like a dog, but feed and clothe him well, work him moderately, surround him with physical comfort, and dreams of freedom intrude. Give him a bad master, and he aspires to a good master, give him a good master, and he wishes for his own master (20).

In many earlier American history textbooks, the newly freed Black man was pictured as bewildered by freedom, a tool of the Northern Carpetbaggers, and unsuited to vote or hold office. After the Civil War, there were 4,000,000 Blacks who were without experience in public affairs. Lincoln had hoped that many Blacks would choose to emigrate from the United States. When he realized that the problem could not be solved in this way, he permitted the establishment of the departments of Negro Affairs. The Freedmen's Bureau grew out of the work of these departments. The Freedmen's Bureau undertook to resettle many people who had been displaced during the war. The Bureau sought to protect the Negro in his freedom to choose his own employer and to work at a fair wage. When it was felt that the interests of Blacks could not be safely entrusted to local courts, the Bureau organized Freedmen's Courts and boards of arbitration. The Bureau achieved its greatest success in education (Johnson 1911).

The majority of new Black legislators were honest and able. Black sheriffs enforced local law. Black lieutenant governors served in South Carolina, Mississippi, and Louisiana. The Black mayor of Natchez ruled White and Black with an evenhanded justice. Eight (8) of the southern states elected Blacks to Congress in the years after the Civil War (Johnson 1911).

Though slavery had been abolished, antebellum attitudes toward the Afro-American continued to influence postwar literature. Like their historian counterparts, White American novelists, short story writers and poets practiced a literary paternalism that encouraged perpetuation of traditional slave characterizations. Indeed, the stereotyped persisted for over a century, prompting one scholar to lament in 1970: We do not know how to portray the black man because there is no tradition of his adequate portrayal" (Van Deburg 89).

However, the Harlem Renaissance, though one may not agree with the characterization of many of the subjects of these literary works, gave many blacks an opportunity to have their literary works read and heard by diverse groups of people.

From 1920 to about 1930, an unprecedented outburst of creative activity among African Americans occurred in all fields of art. Beginning as a series of literary discussions in the lower Manhattan (Greenwich Village) and upper Manhattan (Harlem,) sections of New York City, the African-American cultural movement became known as "The New Negro Movement" and later as the Harlem Renaissance. More than a literary movement and more than a social revolt against racism, the Harlem Renaissance exalted the unique culture of African-Americans and redefined African-American expression. African Americans were encouraged to celebrate their he4ritage and to become "The New Negro," a term coined in 1925 by sociologist and critic Alain LeRoy Locke.

One of the factors contributing to the rise of the Harlem Renaissance was the great migration of African Americans to northern cities (such as New York City, Chicago, and Washington, D.C.) between 1919 and 1926. In his influential book *The New Negro* (1925), Locke described the northward migration of blacks as "something like a spiritual emancipation." Black urban migration, combined with trends in American society as a whole toward experimentation during the 1920s, and the rise of radical black intellectuals—including Locke, Marcus Garvey, founder of the Universal Negro Improvement Association (UNIA), and W.E.B. DuBois, editor of *The Crisis* magazine—all contributed to the particular styles and unprecedented success of black artists during the Harlem Renaissance period.

One of the most controversial writers during this period was Zora Neale Hurston. Although she was criticized my many of her contemporaries such as Richard Wright and Langston Hughes, American history textbooks should recognize her as a literary giant, not only because of her contributions to literature, but also because of her contributions to the evolution of women in literature.

Carl Sandburg praised Zora Neale Hurston as one of the best writer of her era, the 1920s and 30s. An innovator and rebel, her writing provided the inspiration for numerous contemporary writers. One of these, Alice Walker, unearthed her unmarked burial placed and in an essay entitles "In Search of Zora" tried to resuscitate a reputation ruined by the accusation that she had sodomized a ten year old boy (The case was dismissed) and Richard Wright's opposition to the "minstrel" character she used to express her belief that integration was not the answer to the problems of Blacks. Walker felt Zora was digging deeper and more positively into the African-American culture than Wright and other Black opinion makers gave her credit for. The revived interest in Hurston in the late 1960s to the recent recognition of *Their Eyes Were Watching God* as an important American novel has earned both author and novel a position of prominence in the American literary canon.

Harold Bloom, editor and author of several books about the life and works of Hurston believes that *Their Eyes Were Watching* God is a superb and moving novel, unique not in its kind, but in its isolated excellence among other stories of the kind. He states that the "wistful opening" of *Their Eyes Were Watching God* pragmatically affirms greater repression in women as opposed to men, by which I mean "repression" only in Freud's sense: unconscious yet purposeful forgetting" (1).

Now women forget all these things they don't want to   remember, and remember everything they don   want to forget. The dream is the truth. Then they act and do things accordingly (Hurston, 1).

He believes that Hurston's rhetorical strength, even in *Their Eyes Were Watching* God is frequently too overt and threatens excess, when contrasted with the painful simplicity of her narrative line and the reductive tendency at work in all her characters except for Janie and Nanny.   Yet the excess works, partly because Hurston is so considerable and knowing mythologist (2).

Barbara Christian views Hurston's works as traditional from the image of the tragic mulatto to a complex view of black womanhood. She suggests, " Woman, Viewing and Viewed, is part of the theme of Their Eyes Were Watching God, as if the writer were illuminating one part of a canvas in order to give meaning to the entire painting." She concludes that Hurston moved the image of the black woman beyond stereotype. She grated on the 19th century mode a new way of looking at the mulatto and the southern black woman (20).

Nellie McKay believes that Their Eyes Were Watching God offers an opportunity to examine the autobiographical impulse from the perspective of Author Hurston, the writerly self, and fictional Janie, the speakerly self, creating a common text delineating a black female self in writing (51).

In their combined oral and written narrative, Hurston and Janie reinforce Janet Varner Gunn's theory of the autobiographer as self-reader, writing (and speaking) from the "outside in, not inside out or in other words, from the position of the other
side of [the] lived past which the reader self occupies "at the time of writing (51).
In this paradigm, Gunn expands the boundaries of "reader" and "reading" to make the reader not only one person," but also of "position" permitting the observer par excellence the main character in narrator, author, and reader of his or her book like
life; and to make reading an interpretative activity in which "clear and certain knowledge of determinate meanings" gives way to contingent historical experience" and "richer depth in human significance" (51).

From the beginning, McKay asserts, scholars of Afro American autobiography have been in general agreement on the extent to which social and cultural forces influence Afro American identity. Textual evidence shows that, in the face of various oppressions, the black self achieves a wholesome identity through awareness and acceptance of interdependence between the individual and his or her supportive community and the knowledge that collective black American physical and psychological survival depends on the union (even when troubled) of the individual and group.   In respect, the Afro-American autobiographer writes not from internal position of isolated selfhood, but from having to interpret, to read the self ,if you will (as writer and reader of the text), through preexisting layers of group social acculturation that empower and shape that individual self (52). McKay believes that *Their Eyes Were Watching God*, Janie's story, simultaneously written and told, emerges as a composite "reading" of black female growth and development against the history of the oppression of race and sex. This narrative, Mckay concludes, enforces the cultural approach to identity that has dominated the Afro-American male-centered tradition from the slave narrative of the 19th century to the present time, but is also makes of the "autobiographical situation" another vehicle for the
self-empowerment of black women (53).

Alice Fannin asserts that both Janie (Hurston's protagonist in *Their Eyes Were Watching God)* and Celie (Alice Walker's protagonist in *The*

Color Purple) go beyond the traditional levels of the questing female character to arrive at "an exploratum of self as part of the universe as part of the self." She suggests that "Both
women first endure a series of trials which threaten psychic extinction, death in life; both are moved by another person's love as a catalyst to begin to love and value themselves; yet, both finally attain the self-worth necessary to survive alone."

Elizabeth Meese asserts that in the novel *Their Eyes Were Watching God*, "Hurston employs a narrative strategy that is culturally, philosophically, and aesthetically complex." She believes the complexity arises from "Hurston's decision to retell the story rather than to tell it." She contends that "Hurston's aim is textuality, the process of product in a text through the transformation of other texts and through this textuality, a form of feminist self-definition. By transforming Janie's morality, Hurston's intertexts into textuality, the writer creates both herself as a writer and her own story, while Janie creates her life through language." She finds Janie's return as a "speaking subject" significant. She suggests that "By chronicling Janie's development, Hurston transforms the status of narrative from the temporality characteristic of oral tradition to the more enduring textuality required to outwit time's effect on memory. In doing so, she presents feminist readers with a map of a woman's personal resistance to patriarchy and feminist writers in particular Alice Walker with the intertext for later feminist works."

Cyrena Pondrom calls Their *Eyes Were Watching God* "a modern reinterpretation of the ancient Babylonia myth of Ishtar and Tammuz, with syncretic allusion to its analogues, the Greek story of Aphrodite and Adonis and the Egyptian tale of Isis and Osiris." She reconsiders the novel in light of these myths to clarify Hurston's use of folklore, manipulation of narrative viewpoint, attitude toward Western religious values and perspective on black and white relations. She adds that such an approach "offers new evidence concerning Hurston's relationship to the modernist movement." She suggests that Hurston's "adoption of myth as a principle meaning and order is Hurston's most important link to modernism . . . She shares with Eliot, Yeats, Joyce, Pound, and Crane, the use of myth as 'a way of controlling, or ordering, of giving a shape and a significance to the immense panorama of futility and anarchy which is contemporary history.'"

Robert Stepto asserts that before *Invisible Man* , Hurston's *Their Eyes Were Watching God* is quite likely the only truly coherent narrative of both ascent, and immersion, primarily because her effort to create a particular kind of questing heroine liberates her from the task (the compulsion, perhaps) of revoicing many of the traditional troupes of ascent and immersion. He asserts that Hurston is neither entirely new nor "feminine." The house "full ah thoughts" to which Janie ascends after her ritualized journey of immersion with Tea Cake into the "muck" of the Everglades (recall here DuBois's study swamp in both The Souls, The Quest of the Silver Fleece) is clearly a private ritual ground, akin in construction if not in accouterment to DuBois's study (6).

Still, Stepto believes that there is much that is new in *Their Eyes Were Watching* God. The narrative takes place in a seemingly ahistorical world: The spanking new all black town is meticulously bereft of former slave cabins; there are no railroad trains, above or underground, with or without Jim Crow cars. Matt's mule is a bond with and catalyst for distinct tribal memories and ritual, but these do not include the hollow slogan, "forty acres and a mule"; Janie seeks freedom, selfhood, voice, and "living" but is hardly guided or haunted by Sojourner Truth, or Harriet Tubman, let alone Frederick Douglass. Furthermore, Stepto believes that the narrative's frame the conversation "in the present" between Janie and Pheoby creates something new in that it, and not the tale, is Hurston's vehicle for presenting the communal and possibly archetypal aspects of Janie's quest and final posture (6).

Stepto believes that the one great flaw in *Their Eyes Were Watching God* involves not the framing of the dialogue, but Janie's tale itself. Through the frame, Hurston creates the essential allusion that Janie has achieved her voice (along with everything
else), and that she has even wrested from men folk some control of the tribal posture of the storyteller. He asserts that the tale undercuts much of this, not because of its content indeed episodes such as the one in which Janie verbally abuses Jody in public abets Hurston's strategy but because of narration. Hurston's curious insistence on having Janie's tale her personal history in and as a literary form told by an omniscient third person, rather than by a first person narrator, implies that Janie has not really won her voice and self after all that her author (who is quite likely the omniscient narrating voice) cannot see her way clear to giving Janie her voice outright (7).

Lorraine Bethel believes that *Their Eyes Were Watching God* exemplifies the immense potential contained in the Black female literary tradition for the resolution of critical aesthetic and political problems common to both the Afro-American and the American literary traditions. She asserts that foremost among these problems is the question of how Black/Female writers can create a body of literature capable of capturing the political and cultural realities of their experience while using literary forms created by and for white, upper-class men. She believes that Hurston's novel *Their Eyes Were Watching God* offers an excellent source for demonstrating the value of an interdisciplinary approach to Black female literary tradition in particular. She asserts that Hurston locates her fiction firmly in Black women's traditional culture as developed and displayed through music and song. She believes in presenting Janie's story as a narrative related by herself to her best Black woman friend, Pheoby, Hurston is able to draw upon the rich oral legacy of Black female storytelling and myth making that has its roots in Afro-American culture (9-12).

Bethel asserts that the obstacles are conveyed in *Their Eyes Were Watching God* partially through Hurston's use of symbolic geography. Janie's lyric vision is conceived outdoors, in her grandmother's "garden field." When Janie goes inside the house, she reaches "the narrow hallway" and remembers that her grandmother is home with a sick headache." As soon as she is outside, Janie asks herself where the "singing bees" of her lyric vision are and we are told that "nothing on the place nor in her grandma's house answered her. She searched as much of the world as she could from the top of the front steps and then went on down to the front gate and leaned over to gaze up and down the road. Looking, waiting, breathing short with patience. Waiting for the world to be made. "Missy Kubitscheck believes the quest motif structures the entire novel: Janie twice leaves established social positions for a more adventurous life, descends into the underworld of the hurricane, faces a literal trial following Tea Cake's death, and returns to Eatonville with her hard-won knowledge. Indeed. Kubitscheck believes that only very lately have critics allowed Janie to be the heroine of her own story, much less the successful quester returning with a boon for her community. Attacking the tradition of such limiting criticism as "intellectual lynching (20).

Mary Helen Washington has led the way in reasserting the centrality of Janie's search for identity and her connections to her community. Washington argues that the novel's most powerful theme "is Janie's search for identity, an identity which finally begins to take shape as she throws off the false images which have been thrust upon her because she is both black and woman in a society where neither is allowed to exist naturally and freely." Hurston expresses this theme, Washington maintains, through the images of the horizon and the pear tree, the former symbolizing Janie's personal individual quest, and the latter, her search for fulfillment through union with another (60).

Robert Hemenway, author of Zora *Neale* Hurston: *A Literary*

Biography, explores what he terms the personal dimension in *Their Eyes Were Watching God*, Hemenway disputes claims concerning Hurston's relationship with white patrons which insist that she was more comfortable under these arrangements than many of her Negro contemporaries (34).

Hemenway believes that Zora Neale Hurston could not write creatively while under the influence of personal patronage because between November 1926 and August 1933--seven years coinciding almost exactly to the patronage period--Hurston published no fiction. In the decade following the final break with Mrs. Mason, Hurston published six of her seven books, a long series of essays in Nancy Cunards *Negro,* and a large number of reviews, short stories, and essays. Something about being on her own even if it meant scrambling for every hard-earned dollar, liberated Hurston's imagination (35).

He suggests that what patronage did for Zora Neale Hurston was to force her to define the role of black folklore in her life and in her fiction much more clearly than she had ever done before. Patronage made Hurston self-conscious about her role as the dramatist for something unique about the black American experience the rich folklore of the rural black Southerners (36).

He asserts that time after time in *Their Eyes Were Watching* God, Hurston tries represent the difference of blackness through a representation of the folk process. That is why talking buzzards, a ceremonial yellow mule, big picture talkers on Joe Clark's porch, Bahamian Fire Dancers, and lying sessions in the Muck appear so frequently (44).

He concludes that as is usual with black artists in America, the personal dimension to such a magnificent work of fiction turns out to be very complicated (45).

The review in the December issue of *Publisher's Weekly* of the tape of Ruby Dee's reading of Hurston's *Their Eyes Were Watching God* indicates that the novel is newly invigorated. The actress, according to the review, seems able to call forth the characters from a place deep inside her. In all, the reviewers believe that the tape succeeds in its rich descriptions and freshness of dialogue, delivering in terms that are alternately funny and moving (44).

Rachel DuPlessis asserts that the first time we see the heroine of *Their Eyes Were* Watching God, she is sauntering down the road, the knowing subject of gossiping judgment. She concludes that Janie is an expressively sexual woman (her buttocks and "pugnacious breasts" are immediately mentioned). She is black, asserts DuPlessis, but her "great rope of black hair" operates as a marker of her racial mix, and an

evocation of the internal color lines in the African-American community. Janie is forty-- too old according to her neighbors, collectively termed "Mouth-Almighty," to change,
adventure, or express sexuality. Finally, Janie's overalls area nice bit of cross-dressing, signifying equality and sexuality in gender terms, and in class terms signifying her double class status as property (petty-bourgeois - local notable) annealed to "poverty"
(agricultural day worker). These signs, DuPlessis asserts, are constructed by Hurston to be conflictual and heterogeneous in the array of race, gender role, age, class, and sexual markers (95).

DuPlessis suggests that the paradox of Janie-- her fascination--is Hurston's narrating Janie's efforts to spell her life with more than that one word "colored," while necessarily her life is focused by the social, economic and cultural meanings of blackness (95).

Janie, asserts DuPlessis, is an incessant dialogue with the meanings of "colored," of which she is not in control. To construct Janie's dialogue, DuPlessis believes that Hurston has treated many of these social determinants (such as class, sexuality, and gender role) as if they were matters of choice and risk for her character, not fixed and immobilized (96).

Hurston's basic attitude, according to DuPlessis, is that "my race is part of the hand I have been dealt; now I will play it." DuPlessis believes that Hurston wants to analyze race without being reduced to race (96).

DuPlessis asserts that a white critic looking at Hurston could see her Negro ness as marked, and will want to elaborate her attitudes toward that race in isolation from all other factors, including the critic's own assumptions about blackness and whiteness (98).

Hurston, according to DuPlessis, was continually trying to prove that it was always the specificity of individuals that mattered and not their race (DT 238-248). DuPlessis asserts that Hurston had a very complex and conflictual picture of her "Negroness" first as a material fact of course involving social prejudice, which it was in her interest and in her capacity to transcend (98).

Their Eyes Were Watching God was structured in such a way as to reserve judgment most particularly to or for whoever might be construed as "the Negro farthest down" in any situation (DT 177).

The most melodramatic and satisfying moment, according to DuPlessis occurs in the notable confrontation of Joe by Janie is an exchange that ends with her decisive remark, "you look lak de change uh life (75).

Their Eyes Were Watching God, DuPlessis asserts, that any kind of bullying is undercut by whoever is a "cut under": Sop-de-Bottom and Tea Cake undercut Mis Turner; Janie undercuts Joe; mules undercut men (101).

One must begin thinking through the trial scene, concludes DuPlessis, by recalling that after the hurricane Tea Cake and Janie decide to return to the muck, on the principle laughingly discussed, that whites who know you are better than the whites who don't because of the structure of prejudice brought down to its basic component -- prejudgment (102).

The critical reviews of Hurston's Their *Eyes Were Watching God* are numerous and varied; yet, I have found a common thread that runs through those reviews.   It is the acknowledgement that Zora Neal Hurston, through her writings, has left an indelible footprint on the sands of American literary history.

Their Eyes Were Watching God has been read, analyzed, and discussed more by literary critics during the last fifteen years than it was read during its initial publication more than fifty years ago. If textbook publishers were true to history, students would be given the opportunity to learn more about writers such as Hurston. Also, if Hurston had been included in early American history textbook, certainly an in depth review of the importance of *Their Eyes Were Watching God* would have been justified. Since this was not a reality, I have included a review for students of Hurston and students in general to critique.

FROM THE OLD SOUTH TO THE NEW SOUTH TO THE OLD SOUTH

In addition to their influence of postwar literature, antebellum attitudes also influenced the economic conditions of Blacks. The economy put free African Americans at the mercy of local Whites. There were simply too few persons of color for them to trade principally among themselves. They were scattered too widely across the states, with the exception of Charleston, to make extensive trade practical (Johnson 56).

Most free persons of color in South Carolina were poor. In 1860, the mean total wealth per Negro household was $644, one-fifteenth the mean wealth of White families, which was over $10,000. However, most Negroes were even poorer than the mean value suggests (Johnson 59).

The ghettorization of the Black community is both an economic and political reality.   The general state of political and economic subordination is obvious and unarguable.   The only question is the character and process of exploitation and oppression of the ghetto, which has been summed up by many as domestic colonialism. As early as 1962, in an article printed in an earlier book, Cruse (1968) used the category "domestic colonialism" to discuss Black-White relations in the United States Society. He argued that "from the beginning the African-American has existed as a colonial being.... The only factor which differentiates the Afro-American 's status from that of a pure colonial status is that his position is maintained in the `home country's in close proximity to the dominant racial group.

Moreover, a continuous drain of financial, physical, and human resources mark the ghetto economy. The savings are placed in financial institutions whose loans are primarily made to enterprises outside the ghetto. In addition, Blacks pay more than 50 of their income on rent compared to less than 50% by others and most of that is to outside owners. Finally, there is a low-level of repairs and renewal of physical plants in the ghetto and better-educated Blacks with higher salaries tend to move out, thus depriving the ghetto of persons whose education, income, and initiative would be valuable to its revitalization and organized efforts to free itself. "It is in such context of oppression, exploitation and relative powerlessness, that the colonial analogy seems to be a definitive one (Tabb, 1970).

Earlier American history textbooks failed to mention why job opportunities seemed to have eluded Black youth. Increases in concentration of urban poverty among blacks has been especially damaging to the opportunities available for Black youths. Highly concentrated poverty areas can be distinguished from other areas not merely by the race of the residents, but, more importantly, by the kinds of access that the residents of these neighborhoods have to jobs and job networks, availability of marriageable partners, involvement in quality schools, and exposure to conventional role models (Wilson, 1987).

It is well- documented that earlier American history textbooks omitted or distorted information about African-American history from slavery to freedom; yet, more recent American history textbooks include painful facts about the so-called New South.

Chet Fuller, a brilliant young Black reporter for the *Atlanta Journal*, disguised himself as an unskilled, drifting laborer, and slipped into the lower depths of the New South. From the dilapidated farmhouses to the shanty rows in the big towns, he persuaded people to tell him about their lives. He discovered many new insights and old nightmares.

He settled in Charlotte, North Carolina and started searching through the papers for work, but he would find nothing for an unskilled laborer. Job opportunities in the New South were similar to those in the Old South.

Furthermore, the family economic status for Black families in the New South was similar to those in the Old South. Even though a Black man he met during his travels owned his own home, it stayed "tied up in debt" (Fuller 21).

Some Black farmers made a little money farming in the New South, but they were forced to go into debt just to buy food. Most of the Black families in the New South worked from sunup to sundown as their ancestors had done during slavery. The major difference was that the Black farmers in the New South were told that they could own their own land; however, it was highly mortgaged.

Although it was the New South, when Chet Fuller went into a service station for help in repairing his car, he felt as if he needed a gun because he did not know if he were going to be shot. He felt as if his life was in jeopardy. He felt frightened because they fit the stereotyped of "the low-life redneck crackers I had grown up fearing and hating. In all the stories I had been raised on, these ghastly figures continually raping, lynching, castrating, or killing poor, unsuspecting Black men and women--even children--and never having to pay for their dirty deed." "Even after the Civil Rights Movement, the Voting Rights Act, all the things that were supposed to help remove the veil of ignorance and darkness from the South--I still did not feel safe traveling alone in a car in my native region. And no other Black person I knew felt any safer" (Fuller 35). The way in which Black people lived in the Old South and New South was not accurately portrayed in earlier American history textbooks.

The New South, according to Fuller, was "in pretty bad shape, with rotting wood porches and peeling paint." He had seen children playing on the porches and in the yards of dilapidated houses that had paper tags nailed beside the front doors announcing that the houses had been condemned by the city (Fuller 37).

Fuller knew that the new south was similar to the Old South. He said that anything could happen on those streets, where some people lived in houses that had been condemned, where burglaries were as common as rats, where locks were torn "slamp off" doors, where police protection was lax, and where those poor people trying to live quiet lives were easy victims for thugs. There was no place for them to go; the low-rent housing projects were no better. Security and police protection cost money, and they did not have it (Fuller 39).

Fuller concluded that things are going to get much worse for the underclass in this country. "It is hard to accept the fact that for many of those I saw languishing on America's back door steps, the road out of despair is getting longer and more difficult. Still, it is not yet totally dark because a few determined souls manage to find their way safely, every once in a while. They are the lucky ones." . . ."And because there is always God, there is always hope" (Fuller 255).

White response to Black Freedom was one (1) of fear and hatred. Black Codes that replaced Slave Codes restricted blacks. Lacking economic power and therefore at the mercy of his employer, the Black man was dependent on federal forces for protection (Johnson 1911).

In summary, Blacks had been contributing to the success of America from the very beginning. Excluding Blacks from American history had been like excluding Japanese-Americans, Mexican-Americans, Native Americans, Italian-Americans, and Asian Americans from American history. There were several facts about Blacks and their history that were not mentioned in earlier American history textbooks. Blacks accompanied many explorers. Blacks in the early seventeenth century were not slaves but indentured servants. Blacks participated in wars against the French and Indians. Blacks participated in the Civil War. Free Blacks started their own schools. Blacks were not content in being slaves. These facts about Blacks and their contributions were a part of American history. Blacks were freed after the Civil War, and many of them became honest and able legislators. Because many of the Blacks had limited job skills, and were economically poor, they were forced to return to a kind of legalized slavery.

At the beginning of the African presence in the Americas, an African-American culture, nationality and consciousness were constructed. Against great odds, inside the oppressive context of slavery and later racial segregation, the racial identity and perspective of resistance, a community empowered by imagination, was developed against the weight of institutional racism. That historic leap of collective self-definition and inner faith must once again occur, now inside the very different environment of mature capitalism. We must begin the process of redefining blackness in a manner, which not only interprets but also transforms our world (Marable 9-10).

CHAPTER III

A CONTENT ANALYSIS OF TWO (2) GENERAL AMERICAN HISTORY TEXTBOOKS TO EXAMINE THE PRESENCE OF THE AFRICAN AMERICAN

Content analysis is the process of systematically determining the characteristics of a body of material-books-techniques—events of an era—from frequency counts on words of a certain kind to analysis of plot. Findings through content analysis are based on knowledge rather than theory.

The African-American image in the 1968 edition of the textbook *Rise of the American Nation* was extremely different than his image in the 1982 edition of this textbook. The differences in the African-American presence during this span of fourteen (14) years were the basis of comparing the two (2) general American history textbooks.

Attitudes of influential personalities in the system, the structure and condition of the system, domestic needs, public opinion, specific group interests, organizational needs, values, and traditions were the factors addressed in this comparison of the two (2) textbooks.

Personalities in the System

In 1968, after the death of Dr. Martin Luther King, Jr., many thought that the Civil Rights Movement had lost momentum. Certain personalities in society thought that this death would change things for African Americans. Many governors, mayors, congresspersons and senators thought America would be the way it was before the Civil Rights Act of 1964. These attitudes were reflected in the 1968 edition of *Rise of the American Nation*. The governors in the South were influential in society, and their actions and beliefs seemed to have been given more attention on the few brief pages about the African American's struggle than the actual struggle. In the 1968 edition of *Rise of the American Nation*, the authors stated that Governor George Wallace of Alabama and Governor Ross Barnett of Mississippi would rather close the schools in their state than to have them integrated. Governor Lester Maddox of Georgia said that he would not allow Blacks in the schools in Georgia. Paragraphs were devoted to the beliefs and actions of these governors, but only a few short lines were devoted to the beliefs and actions of African Americans. On the other hand, the 1982 edition of *Rise of the American Nation* gave the pros and cons of the African American's struggle for equality throughout this edition. The 1982 edition of *Rise of the American Nation* did not isolate the African American's struggle on six (6) pages as perhaps the 1968 edition did.

President Lyndon Johnson was not given any more attention in the 1968 edition of *Rise of the American Nation* than the governors of Alabama and Mississippi. President Johnson's signing of the Civil Rights Act of 1964 was a significant act in history, but it was treated in four (4) paragraphs in the 1968 edition of the textbook *Rise of the American*

Nation. Because some governors, senators, congresspersons, and other influential people in society did not recognize the African American's struggle as a major one in American history, it was not treated as such.

As more senators, congresspersons, and governors began to realize that any American's denial of freedom jeopardized their own freedom, attitudes began to change. These changes were reflected in the 1982 edition of *Rise of the American Nation.* The attitudes of influential personalities in the 1982 edition included African Americans, Whites, Native Americans, Chinese and all other nationalities that had helped make America a great nation.

Julian bond, a former Congressperson from Georgia, whose views were not mentioned in the 1968 edition of Rise of the American Nation stated the following in the 1982 edition: "Blacks wear their battle scars proudly, and we will continue to move to obtain the right to a decent life where our culture, our beauty, and our soul can be reflected" (24).

The Structure and Condition of the System

The structure and condition of the system had its impact on American history textbook publishers. The American system perpetuated the belief that African Americans were inferior to Whites. This nation was founded with the help of many nationalities, but only a few were given credit for their deeds in earlier American history textbooks. American history textbook publishers were victims of a society that feared that the truth about the building of this nation would alter the structure of the system. Consequently, the 1968 edition of *Rise of the American Nation* treated slavery as an institution that was a natural part of society. However, the 1982 edition of this same American history textbook reflected the changes in the structure of American Society. The publishers began this edition with the Native American, a people seldom credited with helping build this nation, and moved on to tell how Africans were taken from their homeland and made slaves in an alien land. Because people were interested in learning the truth about the building of this nation, these history textbook publishers included information about slavery and the African American's contribution to this society that had never been included before.

The 1982 edition of *Rise of the American Nation* included pictures of slave ships, slave auctions, and slave revolts that were not included in the 1968 edition of *Rise of the American Nation.* It also included speeches made by African Americans during and after slavery.

One societal bias that adversely affected the presence of African Americans in many early American history textbooks is the stereotypical perception that education in general and specifically for blacks was insignificant.   Educators are responsible for developing minds and creating leaders, and the best minds are needed for these enormous yet challenging tasks.

Because it was against the law to teach slaves to read, subsequent generations of blacks have put tremendous emphasis on education; however society in general viewed education negatively. Therefore, until recently, minimum funding was appropriated for education. However, President Clinton, Governor Paris Glendending and members of Congress and state and local legislatures have begun to change people's attitudes about the importance of education.

There has always been the perception that nothing good can come from education. This perception is false. Some of our most brilliant minds have been and are educators; for example Dr. Lucille Upshur Kornegay, Dr. Samuel Proctor, Dr. Benjamin Mays, Miss Doris M. Upshur, Mrs. Mildred Green, Dr. Mary McCloud Bethune, Dr. John Dewey, and the author, Dr. Cora Upshur Ransome are former or present educators.

Some of these biases toward education have lowered teacher morale and have contributed to the failure of our educational system to adequately prepare students to compete in a global society. For example, teachers in the United Sates with advanced professional degrees are paid less, on an average, than other professionals of comparable education such as lawyers and doctors.   Therefore, this salary inequity lowers teacher morale and directly affects the student because he or she does not benefit from the teacher's best effort in teaching the class.

Society, in 1968 was not as positive about education as it was in 1982. However, blacks in education were not viewed positively by society if they pursued a career in education.

Although education and blacks in education were not given the respect and attention they deserved in society and American history textbooks, it still remains the most effective system that one can use in preparation to enter society as a competent productive citizen.

 From this country's inception, people, particularly African Americans, have tried to create a better life for themselves and their posterity, and education has been one of   the most successful methods of reaching this goal.

Textbook publishers must know which concepts or practices have failed or succeeded, especially in education, in the past to intelligently plan for the future. According to the evaluation of past American history textbooks, much work has to be done in documenting contributions by the African Americans in the area of education.

Domestic Needs

The differences in domestic needs in the United State in 1968 and 1982 were a primary consideration in this comparison. Some of the major concerns on the home front were civil rights, population explosion, and the economy. These concerns did not seem very different than concerns today, but they were different. Textbook publishers addressed each of these concerns, but the smallest section of the 1968 edition of *Rise of the American Nation* was devoted to civil rights. The 1982 edition focused on Civil Rights, the Energy Crisis, Unemployment, and Labor Unions in the United States. Each of these concerns was addressed from the point of view of many nationalities. The tables in this 1982 edition compared the African-American's rate of employment and salary with that of Whites. This information was significant for African Americans as well as Whites. In the 1968 edition of *Rise of the American Nation,* no African Americans gave their opinions about domestic concerns, not even Civil Rights. On the other hand, the 1982 edition of this textbook gave viewpoints of many African Americans, such as Frederick Douglass, Whitney Young, Malcolm X. and W.E.B. Dubois. These comments made by African Americans hopefully gave all children an understanding of how Blacks felt about important issues.

Specific Group Interests

The viewpoints of specific organizations included in the 1968 edition of *Rise of the American Nation* did not include very much about Black organizations. The National Association for the Advancement of Colored People (NAACP) and the Congress of Racial Equality (CORE) were mentioned, but only in connection with housing. The 1982 edition of *Rise of the American Nation* gave the origin of the National Association for the Advancement of Colored People and the Congress of Racial Equality. This information was an important part of American history.

Specific groups in society were interested in keeping the African American's image distorted and limited. These groups in society had their impact on American history textbook publishers. One of these groups was the Ku Klux Klan. The Ku Klux Klan had as its primary purpose the exclusion of African Americans and other non-Protestant Anglo-Saxon Americans from society. The 1968 edition of *Rise of the American*

Nation mentioned the purposes of the Ku Klux Klan on four (4) different pages. The 1982 edition of *Rise of the American Nation* gave specific information about the Ku Klux Klan. The purpose of the Klan was discussed, but it was also stated that very few influential White Southerners were ever members of the Klan, and its power gradually faded away.

Another group more powerful than the Ku Klux Klan was the labor union. The labor union was discussed in the 1968 edition of *Rise of the American Nation*, but most of the time the African Americans were unemployed. The 1982 edition of *Rise of the American Nation discussed* the labor forces with the African American as a participant in an advocate for higher wages.

Public Opinion

Public opinion was an important consideration for American history textbook publishers. In 1968, there was a feeling of discontent among the public. African Americans were rioting after the death of Dr. Martin Luther King, Jr., and many citizens felt that because the African American was destroying property and causing deaths, he deserved no civil rights. Many congresspersons and senators felt that the African American had gained enough equality when the Civil Rights Bill of 1964 was signed. Many African Americans concluded that there was no hope in gaining equality for African Americans after the death of Dr. Martin Luther King, Jr., and became complacent. The inclusion of the African American's violence in the 1982 edition of *Rise of the American Nation* did not justify the African American's violence, but it gave the reader possible reasons for his or her actions.

Organizational Needs, Values and Traditions

Many organizations in 1968 were interested in keeping the African American's feeling of inferiority intact. Some tennis clubs, golf clubs, and country clubs were trying to keep their membership growing by excluding Blacks. The exclusion of Blacks had been the tradition of some of these clubs down through the ages, and many did not want to change their policy. Some publishing companies felt the pressure coming from these groups, and many of them responded by painting an inferior picture of Blacks in American history textbooks.

The 1982 edition of *Rise of the American Nation* presented evidence of the changes that had taken place in organizational traditions and values. The African American's struggle from slavery to freedom was discussed in depth.

In summary, many factors contributed to the African American's presence in American history textbooks. Personalities in the system, the structure of the system, domestic needs, specific group interests, organizational traditions and values all helped perpetuate the myth that was found in some American history textbooks concerning the African American.

This part of the content analysis examined the presence of the African-American in the discussion of significant subjects such as Early Explorations and Settlement, Race Relations, Role Models, The Black Church, Civil Rights, Slave Revolts, Education, Contributions, the Old South and Inventors in two general American history textbooks: the 1968 edition and the 1982 edition of *Rise of the American Nation.* Then the information was rated on a scale from 1-10 according to its importance or word frequency. 10 represents very important or that the word appeared at least 100 times, and 1 represents unimportant, meaning the word appeared less than 10 times.

Early Explorations and Settlement

Importance

1968	1982
4	1

In addition to the areas previously discussed, the   content   analysis also ex -amine the differences in the discussion of subjects such as Early Explorations and Settlement, Race Relations, Inventors, Role Models, the Black Church, Civil Rights, Slave Revolts, Education, Contributions and the Old South.

None of the information about early explorations and settlement in the 1968 general American history textbook *Rise of the American Nation* mentioned the African American's contributions.   The sentences regarding the African-American's presence in the Americas during early explorations and settlement are in the context of slavery. "For the hard labor in their mines and on their plantations, the Portuguese and Spaniards used many slaves" (14).   Because many Indians died from European diseases or escaped to nearby jungles or mountains during early explorations and settlement, Spaniards and Portuguese began importing Africans to work as slaves in their New world colonies (14-15).

Although the 1982 edition of *Rise of the American Nation* does not mention the African American's contribution in its discussion of early exploration and settlement; however, it does admit in a chapter of the textbook, which focuses on African Americans that blacks contributed to the early explorations, and settlement of America.

Blacks accompanied many of the explorers.   Scholars contended that Columbus' pilot was black.   Balboa brought thirty (30) Blacks with him.   Cortez was accompanied by a black, who finding in his rations of rice some grains of wheat, planted them as an experiment and thereby introduced wheat raising in the Western Hemisphere.   Blacks participated in the exploration of Guatemala and the conquest of Chile, Peru, and Venezuela.   Blacks were with Ayllon in 1526 in his expedition from the Florida peninsula, northward, and took part in the establishment of the settlement of San Miquel, near what is now Jamestown, Virginia.   Blacks accompanied Narvarez on his ill-fated adventure in 1526 to the Southwestern part of the United States.   There Estevencia, a Black, discovered Gibola, "The seven cities" of the Zuni Indians.

Race Relations

Importance

1968	1982
2	7

Race relations are discussed on two pages of the 1968 edition of *Rise of the American Nation,* but it is discussed under the subtopic: "Segregation of the Races."   Black southerners had hoped to share in the agricultural, industrial and educational progress of other New South, and in the nation's ideas of freedom and equality.   Their hopes did not materialize for several reasons.   First, the federal government suspended its program for helping black southerners make the transition from slavery to freedom. Second, and equally important, white Americans in both the North and the south continued to think of black Americans not as equals but as inferiors. Third, since so many Negroes lived in the south, white southerners feared that the white southern way would be threatened if black southerners were not firmly "kept in their place" (373).

Except in a few instances, the Radical Republicans had not tried to bring white and black children together. However, black and white used the same transportation facilities and other public services. The Civil Rights Act of 1875 had declared that "all persons within the jurisdiction of the United States shall be entitled to the full and equal enjoyment of the accommodations, advantage, facilities, and privileges of inns, public conveyances on land or water, theaters and other places of public amusement; subject only to the conditions and limitations established by law and applicable alike to citizens of ever race and color, regardless of any previous condition of servitude" (374).

Even after the white southern rule was restored in 1877, southerners of both races often used the same transportation facilities and other services. In 1877, the Supreme Court ruled against the Civil Rights Act of 1875 on the ground that the Fourteenth Amendment forbade states, not individuals or corporations (such as railroads), from discriminating against black citizens.

In 1881, Tennessee passed the first of the so-called "Jim Crow" laws. Under this law, white southerners and black southerners were unfairly required to ride in separate railway cars. Other states followed Tennessee's example. In 1896, the Supreme Court added legal support to segregation. In the case of Plessy Vs. Ferguson, the Court ruled that it was not a violation of the Fourteenth Amendment to provide "separate but equal facilities for black Americanize. This 1896 ruling of the Supreme Court was a serious blow to the efforts of black Americans to improve their lives.

On the other hand, the 1982 edition of *Rise of the American Nation* addresses race relations in the United States more generously. Eleven pages in the 1982 edition of *Rise of the American Nation* focus primarily on race relations in the United States. In addition, several photographs of well-known blacks such as W.E.B. DuBois, Frederick Douglass and Malcolm X who fought to improve races relations in America are also included in the 1982 edition of this textbook.

As I mentioned earlier, the 1986 Plessy Vs. Ferguson ruling by the supreme court one year after the death of Frederick Douglass was a serious blow to black Americans; however, it alerted them that their fate was in their hands. Consequently, black leaders struck out on their own.

In 1905, W.E.B. Dubois and others met at Niagara Falls in New York. From this meeting came a list of demands and rights including equal job opportunities, and an end to segregation. This call stirred into action some Progressives like the Settlement House worker, Jane Addams, the educator, John Dewey, and the magazine publisher Oswald Garrison Villard (the grandson of abolitionist William Lloyd Garrison). These Progressives joined DuBois in 1910 to create the National Association for the Advancement of Colored People. This organization led the fight for freedom in the 20th century.

Role Models

Importance

1968	1982
2	6

In comparing the frequency of the presence of African-American role models in the 1968 edition and the 1982 edition of *Rise of the American Nation*, I found a disparaging range. The 1968 edition of *Rise of the American Nation* included one line about Duke Ellington, jazz great; four lines about Phillis Wheatley of Massachusetts, which, in summary, stated that she received some education, unlike most slaves, and became one of the best known poets of colonial New England. In addition to Phillis Wheatley, Mary McLeod Bethune is mentioned as one of the prominent leaders who made up President Roosevelt's "black cabinet' (592). Furthermore, A. Phillip Randolph, president of the Brotherhood of sleeping Car Porters' Labor Union, is recognized because he threatened to march on the national capital with 10,000 Negroes to demand equal employment opportunities. Responding to this pressure, President Franklin Roosevelt in June 1941, established the Fair Employment Practices Committee (FEPC) to counteract racial discrimination in industries that were expanding though government contracts to meet wartime needs. Also, Dr. Martin Luther King, Jr., is recognized for his leadership role in the 1950s and 60s Civil rights Movement. One of his greatest efforts for the Movement was his participation in organizing the 1963 march on Washington where he delivered his famous speech, "I Have a Dream." Dr. King is also recognized for his oratory ability in the 1968 edition of *Rise of the American Nation.* Moreover, the 1968 edition of Rise of the American Nation includes a description of Frederick Douglass, a former slave and one of the most effective speakers of the American Anti-slavery Society, and Harriet Tubman, a runaway slave who lead hundreds of slaves to freedom on the "underground railroad."

On the other hand, the 1982 edition of Rise of the American Nation includes several photographs and information about several African-American role models such as Edward A. Johnson, James Meredith, and Soujourner Truth. These African-American role models are mentioned in the context of their unique contribution to America.

Edward A. Johnson, a black textbook author, is shown in the 1982 edition of *Rise of the American Nation* with a page from his *School History of the Negro Race in America.* Studies such as this were part of a growing literature on black Americans. Also, members of a black signal corps that served in the Spanish American War are included in the 1982 edition of *Rise of the American Nation.*

James Meredith, a 29-year-old black Air Force veteran, tried to enroll at the University of Mississippi, a school that had never admitted blacks. Although Meredith was authorized by a court order to enroll, the University refused to admit him. The Justice department then directed the US Circuit Court to order his admission. Meredith is probably one of the most outstanding role models mentioned in the 1982 edition of *Rise of the American Nation* because of his willingness, at a young age, to change the course of history.

Another outstanding African-American role model mentioned in the 1982 edition of Rise of the American Nation is Sojourner Truth, who was born a slave but was freed. She spoke out in defense of blacks and women. In the 1982 edition of R*ise of the American Nation,* Truth is included with Elizabeth Cady Stanton and Susan B. Anthony as one of the leaders of the Women's Movement. Also mentioned in the 1982 edition of *Rise of the American Nation* is Andrew Young, the United States Ambassador to the United Nations during the presidency of Jimmy Carter. Young insisted that Jimmy Carter's American foreign Policy, which was to be guided by a concern for human rights be both morally right and politically effective.

The Black Church

Importance

1968	1982
2	4

The black church has always been a refugee for African Americans. Early in the nation's history, black people formed their own church. In the 1968 edition of Rise *of the American Nation,* the black church is mentioned in the context of colonization and the condemnation of it by free blacks. In contract, the 1982 edition of *Rise of the American Nation* mentions the black church in reference to its significance in the Anti-slavery Movement and the civil Rights Movement.

In the nineteenth century, the black church was instrumental as a meeting place and haven for run-away slaves. It was also a source of comfort and encouragement for African-Americans in their continued stride towards freedom.

The black church sustained blacks collectively by giving them a reason to live amid the adversity and oppression.   The black church obviously began as a spiritual sanctuary and community against the violent and destructive character of the slave world. Even after slavery it remained a wall of defense and comfort against racism and its accompanying attacks on black dignity, relevance and social worth. Secondly, the black church served as an agency of social reorientation and reconstruction, morality and spirituality in the face of the corrosive effects of slavery (Blassingame, 1979). The black church became the first institution to preach and practice collective self-reliance. "The earliest rudiments of the economic mutual development came from the black church. Bishop Richard Allen, founder of the African Methodist Episcopal (A.M.E.) Church, and Absalom Jones, the first black Episcopal priest in the nation, formed the first officially established church" (Jackson 1988).

Civil Rights

Importance

1968	1982
4	9

Civil rights and the black American are mentioned on sixteen (16) pages of the 1968 edition of the American history textbook Rise of the American Nation.

The discussions of civil rights begins with the discussion of slavery and continuous through the 1950s and 60s civil rights Movement.

Negroes, whether free or slave, as a class apart and an inferior class at that. Most were forced to live apart from white colonists and obey special laws enforced by white colonists. Even so, black men and women contributed enormously to the growth of the colonies. White colonists did not expect hard labor from Negroes; they demanded it. Yet, in a new land abounding with opportunity, few black men and women were permitted to work, save, or build better ways of life for themselves or their families (64).

The Thirteenth, Fourteenth and Fifteenth Amendments ratified soon after the Civil war, became constitution al cornerstones for the long and continuing struggle of black citizens to secure equal rights in America. Amendment 13 freed the slaves, Amendment 14, made Negroes citizens, and Amendment 15 forbade the states to deny black Americans the right to vote.

By 1860, about 250,000 free Negroes lived in the South, most of them in towns and cities. Some of them had been firmly established, masters became more and more reluctant to free their slaves. To do so, meant large financial loss and the disapproval of neighbors. At the same time, "free" Negroes in the south enjoyed less and less freedom.

After 1830, the legislatures of all the southern states passed laws severely restricting the movement of free black people. Free Negroes had to register with town authorities and carry a pass to show that they were not runaway slaves. Often, they had to post bonds—money or pledge of property—to guarantee their good behavior. Their property was taxed, but they did not have the right to vote.

Nor, could they testify in court against white citizens or slaves, although slaves as well as white citizens could testify against them.

There was much other discrimination. Free black southerners could not assemble freely for any purpose. In many places, they were forbidden to attend churches, even all-Negro churches, unless a white person was present. Laws in some areas forbade them to learn how to read and write.

Although these sever laws and regulations were not always enforced, free black southerners lived under the constant threat that they might be. In addition, free Negroes never new when some new law or discrimination might be imposed. Also, they never knew when they might be punished or even sold into slavery for some minor violation.

The reluctant admission of black Americans into the Union forces did not mean that they lived and fought on equal terms with white soldiers. Black soldiers were less well trained than white soldiers and received less adequate medical services. They frequently were assigned the menial, nonmilitary chores around camp. Although Negroes served as noncommissioned officers, only a handful received commissions.

Black soldiers were often badly treated, not only by white soldiers but also by northern white civilians. Through most of the war, black soldiers received less pay than white soldiers; some Negro troops, in fact, refused to accept pay at all until this injustice was ended. Finally, after great pressure, Congress, in 1804, provided that "black soldiers were to receive the same as white officers."

Confronted by segregation and denied their political and civil rights, some black Americans became disheartened and migrated to other nearby states, such as Oklahoma and Kansas, or moved to the growing northern cities. Most, however, stayed in the south, and worked to develop their own black communities.   Black southerners strengthened their own churches, lodges, and mutual aid societies, developed their own businesses, and against handicaps, tried to secure an education. Their effort began to produce results. In 1865, only about 5 percent of all Negro adults could read and write. By 1900, more than 50 percent had achieved these basic skills.

Southern Negro leaders also protested the growing pattern of segregation and discrimination, and denial of civil rights guaranteed by the Fourteenth Amendment. On the lecture platform, in churches, in the press, and in conventions, they demanded recognition of their constitutional rights. In 1989, the former black abolitionist Frederick Douglass, now an old man, asked whether "American justice, American liberty, American civilization, American law, and American Christianity could be made to include and protect alike and forever all American citizens and the rights which have been guaranteed to them by the organic and fundamental laws of the land."

By way of contrast, the 1982 edition of *Rise of the American Nation* has twice as many pages devoted to civil rights as the 1968 edition of the same textbook.

The Brown vs. Board of Education of Topeka was the first major victory in the long and difficult fight of black citizens for equality in American life. Many hailed the decision. In some of the Border States, progress was quickly made in carrying out the intent of the law. In much of the South, however, there was strong opposition. The Supreme Court recognized the deep-seated hostility to the decision and did not call for immediate enforcement. Instead, it recommended that the states proceed with "all deliberate speed (724).

Many white southerners resisted the integration of schools. One hundred and one of the South's senators and representatives signed a

"Southern Manifesto" that denounced "Brown" as a clear abuse of judicial power . . . which is destroying the amicable relations between white and Negro races. Of the South's senators, only Lyndon B. Johnson of Texas and Albert Gore and Estes Kefauver of Tennessee refused to sign. Southern blacks were soon faced with a far more immediate enemy in the form of the White Citizens' Councils and increased violence. The White Citizens' Councils, which originated in 1954 in direct response to the Supreme Court decision, stood for continued segregation of the races. They used economic pressure such as mortgage foreclosures, job dismissals, and withdrawal of credit, as well as legal maneuvers to block integration. For a time, they were largely successful. One year after the "Brown" decision, in eight southern states, not a single black child was attending schools with whites.

The information in the 1982 edition of the general American history textbook Rise of the American Nation goes into more detail about civil rights than the 1968 edition of *Rise of the American Nation*. The 1982 edition uses more denotative language in describing the events such as the crisis in Little rock, the Montgomery Bus Boycott, and President Kennedy and Attorney Robert Kennedy's roles in the African American's struggle for civil rights. It candid description of the information is based on fact rather than emotion as perhaps the 1968 edition represents.

The 1982 edition of *Rise of the American Nation* names a free black family, the Ashworths, who lived in Texas. The Ashworths had come to Texas to take up granted to them by the Mexican government. The Ashworths as well as other free black settlers in Texas, owned cattle and even slaves. For a time, they got along fairly well with their white neighbors. However, as the war between the North and South approached, tensions and even fears arose (285). This information is significant because it was not mentioned in the 1968 edition of *Rise of the American Nation*. The 1968 edition of *Rise o the American Nation* appeared reluctant to mention information concerning black Americans with the exception of its relevance to slavery.

Even though black Americans contributed greatly to the building of America, their contributions are always prefaced by phrases such as "former slave," and "black cabinet," or words that indicate that the African American is inferior to white Americans.

Slave Revolts

Importance

1968	1982
5	1

The 1968 edition of *Rise of the American Nation* devotes a couple of paragraphs on two pages to the resistance of slavery. Despite all the efforts to control them, many slaves found ways of resisting slavery. An uprising was said to have been organized in Charleston, South Carolina, in 1822 by Denmark Vesey, a former slave. However, reports of this plot may have rested largely on unfounded fears among white southerners, since no actual act of rebellion took place. Whatever the facts may have been, 37 Negroes were put to death and others were severely punished. As a result of Denmark Vesey's actions, the African Methodist Episcopal Church (A.M.E.) was band from South Carolina for twenty-five years because that black church was   the base of Denmark Vesey's activities.

Nat Turner, who was born on October 2, 1800, led the deadliest slave revolt ever in United States history. The Reverend Nathaniel Turner, who never married or had children, led a slave uprising in Southampton County, Virginia in 1831 because he believed that God had chosen him to slaughter white people and free the slaves. Before troops suppressed it, 60 white people and more than 100 slaves were killed. Turner was captured, brought to trial and hanged. After the rebellion, all southern states tightened their control over black people, free as well as slave.

The 1982 edition of *Rise of the American Nation* discusses, candidly, on five pages, the resistance of slavery. Eyre Crowe's 1852 painting "Slave Market in Richmond, Virginia depicts a romanticized image of a slave sale. In reality, slaves were usually barely clothed and were often in chains (86).

Also, the 1982 edition of *Rise of the American Nation* tells us that despite the threat of punishment, some slaves made annual forays off the plantations to visit family and friends. Others resisted their masters within the confines of the plantation grounds. They held secret meetings, staged work slowdowns, broke tools, feigned illnesses, and set fires.

As a result of this resistance, white southerners created a complicated system of permits for slave travel and patriots to enforce the system.

Believing that literacy would lead to empowerment revolt, masters threatened to prevent slaves from learning to read and write. Additionally, "Southern legislatures passed laws that made it difficult for masters to free their slaves (87).

Education

Importance

1968	**1982**
4	9

The 1968 edition of *Rise of the American Nation* devotes four (4) pages to the education of black Americans .In from the 1820s to the 1860s, the doors of higher education began to the period Twilight received a degree from Middlebury College. A few years later Edward Jones, John be opened—but only slightly—to qualified black students. In 1823, Alexander Russwuum, and John Templeton graduated from Amherst, Bowdoin, and Ohio University.   Three special colleges for black students were established in this period: Avery College and Lincoln college in Pennsylvania, and Wilberforce College in Ohio. However, the only truly co racial as well as coeducational college as Oberlin in Ohio. People who believed in abolition founded Oberlin in 1833.   Out of 8,800 young men and women who attended Oberlin between 1833 and 1861, 245 were black. In 1865, Congress, at the urging of Josephine Griffing, an Ohio abolitionist and women's rights leader of the 1850s created   the   Freedman's Bureau, making it responsible for looking after "refugees, and abandoned land" (360). This was the first important example in the nations' example in the nation's history of the federal support for needy and underprivileged people. General Otis Howard of Maine headed the Freedmen's Bureau. In 1867, General Howard founded Howard University in Washington, D.C., with the primary purpose of offering higher education to the freed slaves. Booker T. Washington and W.E.B. DuBois had different views regarding how blacks should be educated. Washington believed that if Negroes were to survive and improve their lives, they must have job skills and training.   On the other hand, DuBois urged broader educational opportunities, particularly for talented young Negroes. Dubois urged black Americans to demand their rights to have whatever kind of education they needed to achieve full equality and opportunity in American life. The 1982 edition of *Rise of the American Nation* discusses on seven (7) pages, that the education of black Americans was aided in their efforts by the Freedmen's Bureau, an office of the War Department established to provide ex-slaves with food, teachers, legal aid, and other assistance. The bureau also distributed horses, mules, and land that had been confiscated during the war. With the Bureau's help, about 40,000 African Americans were able to establish their own farms in Georgia and South Carolina. Other pages in the 1982 edition of *Rise of the American Nation* discuss civil rights and the Brown vs. Board of Education of Topeka, Kansas, which ruled that segregated schools were unconstitutional. In addition, it discusses Booker T. Washington and W.E. B. DuBois' views of African-American education. Also, Thurgood Marshall's civil rights victories before the Supreme Court are discussed as they related to the education of blacks in America.

If textbook publishers are to be relevant in the 21st century, they must keep abreast of the changes in education, specifically higher education, as it impacts diverse groups, such as the African American.

There are numerous and varied programs that might be used in teaching the so-called minority. However, most of the programs must address the student's culture and its impact on a global society. Because students will be expected to compete will students from various cultures, they must become familiar with these cultures and understand their significance in a changing society. Therefore, the Arts and Sciences curricula should reflect a multicultural approach to learning. In addition, all other disciplines, including Education, should integrate this approach. If these programs are implemented successfully by colleges and universities throughout the globe, then higher education would have fulfilled its goal: to educate a diverse population for the 21st century. And beyond.

The first ethnic studies programs were established at San Francisco State University and the University of California (UC) at Berkeley as a result of massive student strikes in 1968 and 1969. (This information is a part of our history and should be included in American history textbooks.) The Asian students joined forces with other students of color to demand the creation of ethnic studies programs that would highlight the historical and contemporary experiences of nonwhite groups in the United States in order to counter the existing Eurocentric curriculum that either failed to include any information about people of color, or worse, badly distorted the latter's history (Chain and Wang 46).

In terms of location within the university structures, the ethnic studies programs can be grouped under five categories: (1) relatively autonomous programs housed within a larger ethnic studies entity, (2) subunits within preexisting departments, (3) research centers that sponsor a limited number of courses, (4) programs that have a separate office but whose faculty hold joint appointments in disciplinary departments; and (5) scattered courses (or in some instances just a single course) housed in whatever units are willing to accommodate them.

Despite their different organizational settings, Asian-American studies programs like other ethnic studies programs or department have experienced difficulties; with governance, academic legitimacy, professional certification, and educational mission (Colon 47).

If these issues are not effectively solved by the next millennium, minority programs in higher education will only maintain a steady state. Also, diverse groups will have to do more to support one another to infuse cultural democracy into the higher education enterprise. A new dialogue must be struck and functional unity built, for instance, between women's studies ethnic studies if we are to incorporate cultural diversity into gender-related scholarship (Colon 8). Additionally, the crafting of viable infrastructure as a mechanism for ensuring continuity of movement toward democratic cultural pluralism is a task that the various schools associations and agencies must focus.

How can textbook publishers report history accurately without documenting the impact that population changes have had on higher education? First, the white, male, suburban, middle class student no longer represents the majority in the classroom. The diverse population in the higher education classroom also includes African Americans, Hispanics, Native Americans and women. With this change in the complexion of the classroom come changes in the curricula. The curricula must not only address the needs of the white male, but also the needs of the men and women of color, the poor, as well as the female. This change will impact education because some professors will require training in multiculturalism to teach the students in their classes. Moreover, in order for higher education to survive this change preparation should be made in advance; one such preparation would be to establish training for professors in multiculturalism and to implement multicultural curricula throughout the United States in preparation for a global society.

Because the student population in the next millennium will be different, its needs will be different. As the number of nonwhites attending institutions of higher education increases, most colleges and universities are committed to increasing minority representation of their faculties. Such efforts reflect in part the commitment by colleges and universities to expand opportunities for minority scholars. Moreover, the conventional wisdom is that by providing minority students with similar-race role models, and by having such role models provide multiracial perspectives in the appropriate disciplines, the interest, motivation and success of minority students will be enhanced. On the other hand, if a great share of insufficient preparation for entering college, substantial adjustments will be required by the higher education system. Such adjustments will include the necessity to change recruiting policies (perhaps including standards for admission) and to increase the availability of financial aid.

There will be a great deal of interconstitutional competition for students over the next decade, and much of this competition will be for minority students. However, for a given pool of minority students, such competition is a zero-sum game. It would be much more fruitful to work at enlarging the pool. There will be continued competition from the military and from the job market. However, if higher education meets the need of minority students, it will attract them. It is likely that a larger proportion of resources will have to be spent on remediation, that is, unprepared students will have to be brought up to the level where they can deal with college courses. Greater efforts will have to be made to retain them until the completion of the programs in which they enroll.

Based on the age distribution of the population in the US already born and some reasonable assumption about immigration from abroad, it is clear that the eighteen-year-old population available to consider higher education by the year 2000 will be much more ethnically diverse than has been the case historically in the US. It is tempting to place the responsibility on institutions other than those in the postsecondary system such as the family, social services agencies and particularly secondary schools. However, it is likely that whatever improvements are made in those areas, the responsibility for the post-education of our nation's youth will remain with the college and universities of this country. As the nature of the student body changes, this will be a major challenge

Many of the changes in modern education have occurred because of "the closing of the American mind" (Bloom 5). The higher education curricula have failed to address, effectively, the moral and social issues that are needed to produce men and women of taste, knowledge, vision, and integrity to lead us into the next millennium. For example, many students have not been taught to use the higher order thinking skills such as analysis, synthesis, and evaluation effectively; therefore, many of them still function on the rudimentary level of decision-making. Moreover, students have no shared goals or visions that perpetuate a better an more cohesive society.. "Where there is no vision, the people perish" (Proverbs 29:18). Furthermore, many students are not adequately prepared to work with and live in a diverse global population. Men and women of diverse cultural and racial backgrounds are not communicating effectively with one another because there are very few courses in the curricula of higher education that prepare them to do so.

Modern education has moved toward a pattern of openness or a pattern of anything is accepted. For example, students no longer feel that they are responsible for their own education. They expect the professor to give them a grade that they have not earned after they have put forth little effort to succeed. In addition, they do not want to accept responsibility for their behavior. Many students disrespect their classmates and professors and view their behavior as proper because most higher education curricula (although the family is primarily responsible for teaching morals) do not adequately address moral issues. Therefore, the pattern of education has moved away from student accountability and toward moral decline.

What effect has the lack of student accountability and moral decline had on the modern changes in education? These factors have caused educators to rethink their approach to education. They are now trying to develop curricula that will adequately prepare their students for the 21st century. These curricula include specialization courses and a CORE curriculum that prepare the student completely to enter society. However, today's society owes them something rather than a group of people who want to contribute to growth of the individual as well as society. If an individual is not adequately prepared intellectually, socially, and morally to enter society, then society suffers because it lacks competent and productive citizens.

The implications of these changes for modern education are overwhelming. "A new literary genre, cystopia, the opposite of utopia, emerged to warn of the negative future if present trends continue" (Naisbitt 259). "For within the symbolism of the millennium is the apocalyptic battle between good and evil. Will we face the demise of civilization as know it by nuclear accident or the greenhouse effect . . ." "But what if, the language of symbolism, the antichrist has already appeared in the form of the "God is dead" philosophy, in the worship of only science, culminating, in the creation of weapons of mass destruction and untold other ways to destroy our lives and the lives of our neighbors" (Lemonick 59).

The information highway will impact education; therefore, textbook publishers will be required to report the historical facts about this trend of the future and its impact on minorities, especially African Americans.

Because computer technology and software are changing so rapidly, it is essential that modern education stay abreast of the current trends and methods used to facilitate computer-assisted writing. Software programs like Writing Tutor IV for Windows, Grammar Workouts, Learning Plus, Expressways, and Writer's Helper, in conjunction with tools for checking spelling or choosing words from a thesaurus allow users to improve their language and writing skills within the context of their own writing.

The computer can assist students in capitalizing on diverse learning strategies such as peer tutoring, collaborative learning, peer editing, and cooperative learning. "Highly advanced computers will serve as both tutors and libraries, interacting with students individually and giving them access to a universe of information so vast that it will make today's Library of Congress look like a small-town facility (Lemonick 59).

Networks will continue to be relevant to the use of technology in the twenty-first century. As such, textbook publishers will continue to focus on the history of the Technological Age, Technology, as aforementioned, will impact so-called minorities, especially African Americans, more significantly than any other group of people because of access to training in the past practices training and job discriminatory practices. Though others have been earlier in charting the educational implications of networks (e.g., Hiltz, 1986), it was Trent Batson who was the primal scene of networked writing instruction. Ted Batson (1994) wondered if electronic conferencing in the composition classroom (ENFI) would be "the best friend a teacher ever had or the worst nightmare" (p.3)?

I believe that electronic conferencing in the classroom can be the writing teacher's best friend. Most students can learn more in any given span of time than they do with appropriate curricula, pedagogical and technological support. If we as writing teachers can change the attitudes towards literacy and writing in using technology, then we should seize the opportunity to take the lead "as a cultural-change agent" (p. 2).

My primary goal in pursuing this project is to develop a pilot program for the integration of technology (networked computer classroom) into the Composition and Literature classes at Bowie State University.

The motivation behind this project is to show a mark improvement in student writing skills. A technological approach to teaching writing helps students to acquire twenty-first century competencies as well as improve writing skills. Moreover, technology gives students an opportunity to become more active, skilled and self-directed learners, assuming greater responsibility for the pace, style, and sometimes even the content of their learning. Furthermore, students can manipulate and reorder what they learn, giving them greater control over their learning.

The potential impact of the networked computer classroom on the curriculum and Bowie State University in general is limitless. Technology links curriculum with realistic experiences. For example, in using computer networks, students can work together in cooperative learning situations to help solve real problems, typing their education to real-life situations and giving them invaluable learning experiences. In addition, technology compels the curriculum to be more flexible. Teachers can create their own teaching materials. For example, teachers can create materials such as composition topics, research projects, oral reports, and so on that will focus on higher-order thinking skills and problem solving that should be reflected in the curriculum design.

Using the networked classroom to integrate technology into the Composition and Literature classes can serve as a model for integrating technology across the curriculum.

Integrating technology across the curriculum fosters academic and information sharing among diverse populations of students and teachers. This "cutting edge" instructional strategy will ultimately strengthen Bowie State University as a whole and secure its place as a premier University in twenty-first century technological strategies.

In an electronic classroom, the student uses his or her computer to plan, write, revise, and edit his or her writing assignment. Then one of the student's peers analyzes the writing. This approach to editing gives students an opportunity to share ideas and ask questions about the pieces of writing without fear of humiliation. Electronic communication also helps students to analyze each other's work more effectively in a group discussion. In the networked system, peers can talk with each other about their work, and their conversations are recorded under a discussion section. They can go back, if they want, and reread those discussions at a later time. Unlike the oral peer group, where whatever is said is unavailable to the student at a later time, the written discussion is stored on the student's disk, and he or she can retrieve it as needed.

A networked classroom gives students a " deepened sense of community within the classroom" (Hewlett and Pattison 15). Since they critique each other's work many times, they have no fear of sharing their incompetence.

The integration of technology into the Composition and Literature classes will increase students' use of technology as a learning tool and teachers' use of technology as a teaching tool; therefore, the educational environment at Bowie State University will be enhanced because students will be encouraged to interact with one another on a regular basis. Sharing ideas will enable students to improve their writing skills, which will ultimately increase student success in the required English courses and in writing the English Proficiency Examination. Bowie State University will increase its student retention rate and its status in higher education as a premier University in the use of twenty-first century technological strategies.

The integration of technology into the Composition and Literature classes is a student-centered approach. It enables the student to focus on his or her individual needs while fulfilling the objectives of the lesson. By using the computer and a proposed software program, *Connect*, the student can participate in electronic discussion groups and improve his or her writing skills simultaneously.

This study is significant because it will provide invaluable feedback to teachers who integrate technology into course curricula. In addition, it will enhance students' technological skills, writing skills, and interpersonal skills. Students will be able to gather data easily and analyze and synthesize it in new ways. Students will develop higher-order thinking skills and problem solving skills. Students will become more active, skilled and self-directed learners. Student's self-esteem will be enhanced by the equity in distribution of activities. Students will assume greater responsibility for the pace, style and sometimes even the content of their learning. Teachers will become more collaborative, and enhance their technological skills. Moreover, they will become more productive in ideology and in retrieving information.

The workforce will also change in the year 2000, and textbook publishers, curricula committees, and educators need to think seriously about how the information they decide to include in American history textbooks will impact their primary clients, the students (the future employees) and the employers. By the year 2000, a majority of the workforce will be comprised of men and women of color and most of the jobs will be information technology jobs. The advanced capability of computers, and other electronic information software will make Cyberspace the limitless wave of the future.

Hyperspecialization has several significant implications for modern education. " Beyond the first five grade, the standard curriculum will probably disappear. Basic mathematical, reading, and writing skills will still be required of advanced students, along with, for Americans, a solid background in US history and government. But there will be greater specializatation for students who want it. The mass-production approach to the high school diploma will vanish in favor of competency tests in subjects as employers and college admissions officers would then have a much more specific idea of the a student's skills and training (Vinton 72-81).

As a result of revolutionizing education with specialized training, the United States will be able to compete more successfully with competitors such as Japan and the European Community (Lemonick 60).

Since reading is a pre-requisite to understanding the writing process, it is imperative that we discuss the importance of reading as it relates to education.

Effective writing, both the process and the product depends on effective reading. Only by becoming a reader who is critically aware, can one become a self-critical writer who revises and rethinks continually. Only by extending one's reading experienced can one develop new ideas, approaches, and styles for writing.

In addition to the negative comments such as criticism on what is being presented, critical reading also examines the positive aspects. Moreover, it involves analysis, logical reasoning, evaluation, and synthesis, which are higher order thinking skills.

Critical thinking requires some subjectivity, that is, your own opinion. In order to read critically, one should avoid emotional language and generalizations. To illustrate, "Today, at the drop of a dime, a divorce can be arranged." A more effective sentence would be, "Today, a divorce can be attained easily.

Textbook publishers should realize the importance of specific subject matter during the new millennium. The emphasis in education on reading, writing, and thinking skills has come full circle; therefore, textbook publishers must keep abreast of the historical emphasis of education and how the resurgence of this emphasis will impact them in the next millennium.

In addition to avoiding emotional language, one should also avoid generalizations. To demonstrate, it is estimated that millions of dollars can be saved through an implementation of better customer service strategies within the City of Greendale Council. What questions should you ask about this text? What is the specific dollar amount? Millions of dollars is too vague.

Evaluation is one of the higher order thinking skills; therefore, students should be able to read a paragraph critically and actively and evaluate it. To read critically, you need to go beyond what the author is saying; you need to challenge or question that author. In reading actively, you make meaning out of the letters and numbers you encounter in the text. Your mind must be actively engaged with what your eyes see on the page or the computer screen. As you read critically and actively, you need to attend to three different levels of meaning in order to fully understand what you are reading. The three levels are literal meaning, inferred meaning, and evaluated meaning.

In reading for the literal meaning of a piece, the goal is to understand exactly what the author is saying. Once you have grasped the literal meaning, you should go beyond it to the realm of the inferred meaning. Finally, you want to read beyond the literal and inferred meanings to evaluate the significance of a piece's argument. To evaluate is to determine the effectiveness of the piece. Does it include all pertinent information? Is it documented appropriately? Is there any inappropriate information? Has it fulfilled its purpose? Is the diction appropriate? Are the ideas academically sound?

Reading thoroughly on all three levels is crucial to understanding a text well enough to discuss it intelligently and write about it knowledgeably.

Structure your reading process according to the three steps of previewing, reading, and reviewing, and you will understand what you read more completely. One way to ensure that you are reading critically and actively is to annotate the text as you read. Annotating a text means making summary notes in the margins, as well as underlining or highlighting important words and passages. To improve your own writing, you need to engage it critically and actively.

To prepare means to experiment and explore. Decide on a topic, and consider your rhetorical stance, genre, and language choice.

Invent and prewrite. Inventory your knowledge on a topic, prewrite on the topic, and narrow the topic.

Gather information. Work with peers to brainstorm and to discuss your topic. As necessary, find credible sources to support your own ideas.

Plan and organize. To guide your writing, compose a thesis and construct an organizational plan or outline. Try computer pre-writing software. Let your computer's prewriting program help you with the preparation process.

Before you compose, review your pre-writing, thesis statement, and outline, and use them as raw material for your paper.

All in all, critical reading is an extremely valuable method to use in helping students understand the ideas of others. It is a prerequisite to formulating their own responses. When students read critically, they increase their ability to arrive at their own reasons and conclusions. As students learn to compose their own ideas, they also learn how to become better members of an audience.

Improving student writing in the new millennium and beyond will be a requirement of higher education systems; therefore, initiating, implementing and assessing a Writing Across the Curriculum (WAC) program in colleges and universities, particularly Historically Black Colleges and Universities, is inevitable.

Writing Across the Curriculum (WAC) is a phrase, which gained currency in the late 1970's and early 1980's to describe attempts by various colleges and universities to broaden the scope of student writing beyond the confines of English departments. Usually, these programs were initiated by these English departments, but generally, all departments had input into, and control over the ways in which these programs were implemented., The beginnings of WAC are in Britain in the 1960's "language across the curriculum movement" and in ate U.S. in the 1970's with response "by some composition teachers to the media-induced perception of a nation-wide literacy crisis" (Peritz, 2). It should be emphasized that WAC implies an INCREASE in student writing, not a decrease. Because of the large amount of research (in the United States, England and, to a lesser degree, Canada) completed in this area, our WAC initiative has the benefit of years of research into the programs, methods, and evaluation systems of pervious attempts. WAC programs usually consist of faculty from various areas committing to the ideals of WAC theory and then attempting to incorporate writing assignments and/or journals in their classes.

The first question that must be asked is: Why instructors in disciplines that traditionally do not emphasize writing try to get student to write more or to focus more on how they write?

First, there is a widespread awareness that communications skills are crucial in the workforce. If engineering is taken as an example, a survey of 52 US engineering firms indicated that "writing proficiency is a major factor in deciding the promotion potential of an engineer" (Selfe qtd. in Selfe and Arbai 184). Keith Maxwell (who teaches accounting at the University of Puget Sound) assigns case studies regularly to his students and works with them on the clarity of their writing. He says his students are at a significant advantage when they compete for and retain jobs because they have had this experience (Cooke 10). We have all heard the assertion that our students will change jobs at least 3 or 4 times in their careers. Indeed, in Career, Vocational, or Education programs, instructors may be training students for a specific career but may be aware that in five years they may require or desire retraining for a related career or in a completely different field.   Sometimes, in the case of Liberal Studies, Arts, or Sciences students, Bowie State University isn't necessarily training for a specific job niche but rather providing a general education, which prepares the student for a variety of possibilities. In any case, students must have some of the following skills:

I. the ability to solve problems

II. the ability to examine ideas carefully and support them with evidence

III. the ability to incorporate and synthesize information

This proposal is entitled, "The Initiation, Implementation, and Assessment of a Writing Across the Curriculum program at Bowie State University. Bowie State University is a HBCU. This paper will focus on eight components of a Writing Across the Curriculum program.

Component I: Writing Across the Curriculum

Philosophy Statement   and goals

Component II: Composition and Responsibilities of a University WAC Committee

Component III: Specifications for Writing- Intensive Courses

Component IV: Standards for Writing-Intensive Courses by   University WAC committee to guide the process).

Component V: Check List for Writing-Intensive Courses   (used by faculty   preparing a procedure to   teach   writing-intensive courses

Component VI: Request for Approval to Use W-Designation   Cover Sheet   (sample cover sheet for   faculty/department   WAC application) Request for funding

Component VII: Phases of Implementation

Component VIII: Assessment of Writing Across the   Curriculum

Philosophy Statement

Students learn to write by becoming actively involved in the process and product of writing.   If students approach the learning process energetically and seriously, they will be successful.

Writing Intensive Courses at Bowie State University

Because Bowie State University is committed to the improvement of student writing skills, it is the responsibility of all faculties throughout the university to share in this writing commitment. This commitment means that writing must be practiced and reinforced throughout the curriculum.   Students should recognize the importance of writing and speaking   well   or   the   importance of possessing effective communications skills.   Writing assignments must be designed to increase learning by encouraging students to synthesize new knowledge with previous knowledge and to teach discipline-specific uses of writing.

Courses which develop writing skills are of two types: (1) writing courses--those that develop direct instruction in writing skills and the process of writing; and (2) writing-intensive courses--those that have content as their primary focus but also reinforce writing skills by using writing as an integral part of the learning experience.

Goals for Writing-Intensive Courses

1. Use writing as a learning tool to encourage and to reinforce student learning in the disciplines.

2. Assist students in writing more effectively.

3. Use writing as a learning tool to help students learn critical thinking skills.

4. Prepare students for writing in their careers and in their personal and community lives.

5. Encourage literacy across the university.

Criteria for Writing-Intensive Courses at Bowie State University

In designing writing-intensive courses, faculty and departments are urged to be creative and to modify/design courses which are both faithful to the university-wide criteria and reflective of the difference among fields of study. Faculty are urged to determine the specific number and kinds of writing assignments, grading scales, and teaching strategies appropriate for their disciplines and for themselves as individual teachers.

Writing-Intensive Course Requirements

1. Integrate carefully planned writing assignments into the course so that they increase student learning and enhance student ability to write.

2. List the improvement of student writing among the course objectives in the syllabus.

3. Distribute specific written instructions, including criteria for evaluation, evaluation of major assignments.

4. Guide students in conceiving, organizing, and presenting written material in ways appropriate to the subject being studied.

5. Provide an opportunity for students to revise at least one of their writing assignments after receiving response from the professor.
6. Include, with whatever informal or draft writing is appropriate, at least one assignment that requires students to produce finished, edited prose.

6. Consider written assignments as a major part of the final grads; in most cases, this needs to be 50% or more.

7. Distribute writing for the course throughout the semester rather than concentrated at the end.

After discussions, representatives from individual disciplines can make changes in these criteria to meet disciplinary writing needs.

Additional Writing-Intensive Requirements

8. Give attention to both the process and the product of writing. Intervention in the writing process, particularly in its early stages, is a highly effective way of helping students produce better-written work. For example, students can be assisted with task definition, topic selection, information gathering, documentation of sources, organization and formatting, and revision strategies. Major assignments should have clearly defined stages of preparation and regular progress reviews.

9. Provide opportunities for students to consult with instructors and perhaps tutors or one another as they prepare drafts of assignment or revisions.

10. Provide an appropriate variety of writing experiences by including writing; with different audiences, purposes, or formats. They should also be an appropriate mixture of in-class and out-o-class writing and of graded and ungraded writing.

Checklist   for   Writing-Intensive   Courses

1. Are the writing assignments integral parts of the course, rather than exercises that seem tacked on artificially? Are they assignments that promise to enhance student learning?

2. Have you considered various forms of writing such as case studies, laboratory reports, journals, letters, memos, format essays, research articles, project or grant proposals, or other kinds of writing appropriate for your discipline?

3. Does one of your course objectives explicitly mention the improvement of writing?

4. Will you distribute written instruction, including criteria for evaluation, for major assignments?

5. Will students receive guidance in conceiving, organizing, and presenting written material in ways appropriate to the subject being studied?

6. Are there at least two, and preferable more, different writing assignments?

7. Will students revise at least one assignment after receiving your review comments?

8. Does at least one assignment require students to produce finished, edited prose (as distinguished from whatever informal of draft writing you use?)

9. Are written assignment (in-class and out-of-class) worth at least 50%k of the course grade?

10. Do you distribute the writing assignments throughout the course rather than concentrated at the end?

11. Do your statements of departmental responsibility explain how the department will ensure that the writing component is present regardless of who is teaching?

Components of a Teaching Portfolio

Each teacher of an experimental WAC class must select what (s) he considers to be significant pieces of evidence of the nature and benefits of that teaching/learning experience. Although the finished portfolio may contain significant artifact from the course, it must contain the following items.

1. An explanation of the nature of the curse including any distinctive characteristics of the content or students, which would help the UWACC to understand the work of the course;

2. A list of the writing activities which explains the objectives of each activity, the amount of writing required, the frequency and number f writing assignments, opportunities for student revision evaluations standards (for graded writing), and percentage contribution to student's final grad (for graded writing);

3. A copy of the course syllabus/assignment sheets, instructions, or criteria concerning writings that are given out to students.;

4. A cover letter to the committee, which interprets the materials in the portfolio for the committee, explains their relevance, and introduced the faculty member to the committee as a WAC instructor.

WAC Support Services for Students at Bowie State University

I.   Free tutoring

II.   Access to word processing and Internet

III. Workshops in writing, grammar, documentation, and research.

IV.   Faculty "Idea-exchanges."

WAC Faculty

One of the lasting effects of a Writing-Across-the-Curriculum program for the faculty of an institution is the creation of community. This teaching community is made up of individuals who have diverse pedagogical styles and strategies but who share the common goal of improving classroom learning. Teaching in such a program cannot be carried on in isolation but requires group discussion and sharing of techniques, common reexamination of learning methodologies, and working in teaching partnerships. This program provides a forum, very much needed at Bowie State University, where + teachers can regularly can discuss pedagogy and, as almost always happens, make their way across disciplinary boundaries to discover common questions, problems, and solutions. Through the workings of community, Writing-Across-the-Curriculum develops in individual faculty members an introspect and self-aware way of thinking about their teaching which they automatically translate into effective classroom practices.

University Committee Composition and Responsibilities

The University Writing Across the Curriculum Committee will be composed of a faculty who volunteer to serve and are selected and confirmed by the faculty members who volunteer to serve and are selected an faculty of their respective colleges to represent them on the committee. Any faculty members chosen by the colleges to serve must meet the requirements for faculty members who teach writing-intensive, WAC courses and must be designated as WAC faculty. (See "Guidelines for Writing-Intensive Courses.")

Committee members will serve three-year terms, renewable once if selected again by the college for a second three-year term. These terms will be staggered to ensure continuity. The Chair of the University WAC Committee must also meet the requirements for faculty who teach writing-intensive courses. The Chair will serve three-year renewable terms and must be recommended by the committee and approved by the vice-president of Academic Affairs/Provost.

Initially the Committee will be made up of six members representing the College of Liberal Art and at least two members from each f the other colleges. As the program grows and changes, the Vice President o Academic Affairs/Provost will adjust representation accordingly. Rationale: At present over half of the participants in the WAC program are teaching in the college of Liberal Arts.

The University WAC Committee is charged with the following responsibilities:

1. to select those WAC instructors and writing-intensive courses which will fulfill the WAC requirement for all university students, using a clearly defined and well-publicized set f criteria;

2. to make recommendations concerning all aspects of the university WAC program

3. to plan all WAC training workshops and other instructional activities for faculty participants;

4. to make recommendations concerning fair representation of all colleges on the committee as the WAC program grows;

5. to forward current information about Writing Intensive courses to the Vice -President of Academic Affairs/Provost, all academic deans, and the Faculty Senate.

In brief, if textbook publishers are to remain viable, they must keep abreast of all current trends in education in order to meet the needs of their primary customers—students. American history textbooks should also celebrate diversity by focusing on the contributions of all ethnic groups. However, since this book compares the presence of African Americans in American history textbooks, certainly its focus is on the contributions of African Americans

Contributions.

Importance

1968	1982
2	5

The contributions that blacks made to the building of America are not discussed specifically in the 1968 edition of *Rise of the American Nation*; however, blacks are mentioned throughout the textbook. African Americans mentioned in the 1968 edition of *Rise of the American Nation* are A. Phillip Randolph, labor leader, Dr. Martin L. King, Jr., civil rights activist, and Malcom X, social reformist. The contributions of these Americans are not discussed in relation to their significance to America, but what they accomplished in trying to attain rights that had been guaranteed to them as Americans in the Constitution.

For example, A. Phillip Randolph, labor leader, is mentioned in reference to his threat to rally 10,000 Negroes to march on Washington because of the Fair Labor Standards Act did not insure freedom from racial discrimination in employment. However, the significance of Randolph's threat is that President Franklin Roosevelt, in 1941, established the Fair Employment Practices Committee (FEPC), which helped all Americans.

Also, Dr. Martin Luther King, Jr., who certainly helped to make America better for all its citizens, is not viewed from this perspective in the 1968 edition of *Rise of the American Nation*. King, According to the 1968 edition of Rise *of the American Nation* adopted many of his nonviolent view from Henry Thoreau's essay, "Civil Disobedience." However, King published an essay, "Letter From Birmingham Jail," which explains to the Clergy who are questioning his nonviolent techniques, his concept of nonviolence. However, none of King's essays, including "Letter from Birmingham Jail," are mentioned in the 1968 edition of *Rise of the American Nation.* Because Dr. King contributed greatly to the awareness of white America concerning their treatment of black citizens, his works and nonviolent techniques should be included in American history textbooks. The only references to Dr. King in the 1968 edition of R*ise of the Am*er*ican Nation* are of his "I Have a Dream" speech, his influence as a "black leader," and his assassination.

Another black leader mentioned in the 1968 edition of *Rise of the American Nation* is Malcolm X. The references about him, included in two sentences, are of his religious affiliation, Muslim, his beliefs, the transformation of his beliefs and his assassination.

However, the 1982 edition of *Rise of the American* Nation includes a photograph of cowboys taken around 1910. It shows cowhands on a cattle drive. Cowhands, one third of whom were African American or Hispanic American spent time in cattle boomtowns such as Abilene and Dodge City, Kansas. "There they sought relief from the dusty, lonely tracks (117). This information is significant because the 1968 edition of *Rise of the American Nation* does not include, for whatever reason, the black cowboys among their discussion of the exploration of new territories.

Moreover, the 1982 edition of *Rise of the American Nation* shows a lithograph of the firs African Americans who served in Congress: Representative Josiah T. Wall of Florida; Representative Joseph H. Rainy and Representative R. Brown Elliot, both South Carolina, and Benjamin Turner of Alabama.

To summarize, the 1968 edition of *Rise of   the American Nation* shows minimum importance of the history of black Americans and their efforts in making America better for all citizens; however, the 1982 edition of *Rise of the American Nation* mentions groups that included blacks, such as Senators, Representatives and cowboys. The involvement of black Americans in these groups documents the African-American's presence in the pioneering and structuring of America.

Inventors

Importance

1968   1982

1   2

The discussion of black inventors is not significant in the 1968 edition of *Rise of the American Nation*. The total discussion in the 1968 edition of *Rise of the American Nation* mentions one black scientist/inventor, George Washington Carver, under the subheading, "Limited Progress for Negroes states that "George Washington Carver's achievements were truly impressive. In the early 1900s, Carver became famous for his work at Tuskegee Institute in developing hybrid crops and in showing southern farmers, white as well as black, how to increase their crop yields and how to put familiar agricultural products to new uses (579).

However, in the 1982 edition of *Rise of the American Nation,* three black inventors are mentions: George Washington Carver, Eliza McCoy, and J.D. Matzeliger, in reference to the accomplishments of Sidney W. Winslow, President of the United Shoe Machinery Company of Boston. However, if the truth were told, it would state that Matzeliger invented a shoe-lasting machine, which outdated other mechanisms in use. It held the shoe on the lift by a grip, drove nails into place, and delivered the finished shoe in an operation lasting less than a minute. Also, the textbook mentioned that Elijah McCoy who patented an automatic lubricating cup for machines in 1872, which eliminated the need to stop and restart engines in order to lubricate them. His product was so respected that the phrase, "the real McCoy" was used to question or confirm the genuineness of his and other products.

Many of the successes of white inventors were directly attributable to the efforts of black inventors. Therefore, the accomplishments of black inventors should be discussed in all general American history textbooks.

The Old South

Importance

1968	*1982*
4	7

Although the South is discussed in the 1968 edition of *Rise of the American Nation,* it is discussed in the context of slavery, "Jim Crow," laws, civil rights and education. Because slavery was a profitable business, many whites did not want the laws to change regarding it. Because slavery was a profitable business, many whites did not want the laws to change regarding it. Therefore, the Supreme Court, the Legislatures, and whites that were sympathetic to slavery tried to keep this horrific system intact. On the other hand, the 1982 edition of *Rise of the American Nation* allows us to take a peek into this inhumane system. It tells us that blacks resisted slavery from its inception. It discusses abolitionists such as Frederick Douglass, Harriet Tubman, Sojourner Truth, and Lloyd Garrison., who was white, and their contributions to the eradication of slavery. In addition, it informs us that the resistance of slavery went beyond verbal resistance. It included physical resistance in men such as Denmark Vesey and Nat Turner. Moreover, the 1982 edition of *Rise of the American Nation* identifies leaders, not just black leaders, who contributed to the change in laws regarding blacks in

America. Although many of the people who fought and died for justice and equality in the Old South are not mentioned in the 1982 edition of Rise of the American Nation, these people did not die in vain. The Old South may have "Gone with the wind," in reference to slavery, but the bigotry and hatred, in subtle behavior still exist.

To summarize, the purpose of this content analysis was to focus on the presence of African Americans in two general 'American history textbooks: the 1968 edition of *Rise of the American Nation* and the 1982 edition of *Rise of the American Nation*. In the ten topics that were discussed in this analysis, there was a significant difference in the presence of the African American regarding these topics in the 1982 edition of *Rise of the American Nation*. The 1982 edition focuses more on the African American's contribution to America rather than how he or she relates to the African-American race in trying to attain freedom and equality that was guaranteed to him or her by the Constitution. Consequently, the 1982 edition of the textbook rise of the American Nation view African Americans more effectively in the context of Americans rather than black Americans.

Chapter IV

Conclusions and Recommendations

Design of the Study

This study was undertaken to gather information from two (2) general American history textbooks concerning the African-American's image. The 1968 edition and the 1982 edition of Todd And Curti's general American history textbook *Rise of the American Nation* were analyzed. The 1968 edition was published by Harcourt, Brace and World, while the 1982 edition was published by Harcourt, Brace and Javonavich..

Data-Gathering Procedures

A content analysis was made of two (2) general American history textbooks to determine the differences in the portrayal of the African-

American's image. The analysis focused on: (a) attitudes, beliefs, values, and images of influential personalities in the system, (b) the structure and condition of the system, (c) domestic needs, (d) public opinion and specific group interests, and (e) organization needs, values, and traditions. In addition, a content analysis examined several topics such as Early Explorations, Race Relations, Role Models, the Black Church, Civil Rights, Education, Contributions, Inventors, and the Old South, and rated the presentation in the 1968 edition and the 1982 edition of Rise of the American Nation according to their importance.

Analysis of the Data

Data was presented that revealed the distortions and limitations found in earlier published American history textbooks concerning the image of the African American and the improvements made in the African American's image in a later edition of an American history textbook.

Limitations of the Study

The limitations of this study included the following factors: (a) the writer only did the analysis. (b) Its validity and reliability were not tested. However, studies done by the Tennessee, Chicago, and Baltimore School Systems indicate that the self-esteem of African-American students who have seen themselves portrayed positively in general American history textbooks has increased significantly.

Significance of the Study

The findings of this study might facilitate a better understanding of the distortions and limitations concerning the African American's image found in earlier American history textbooks. The findings of this study might educate others about the contributions that the African American has made toward the building of America.

The results of the data-gathering activity might be useful to students during their study of American history.

Although this analysis had its limitations, it might help others such as scholars, textbook publishers, curriculum committees, and students to realize the critical need for diversity in history textbooks.

The findings through content analysis of the 1968 edition of *Rise of the American Nation,* a general American history textbook, reveal significant differences in the African-American presence as it relates to the discussion of subjects such as early exploration and settlement, race relations, role models, the black church, civil rights, slave revolts, education, contributions, inventors, and the old south.

1. None of the information about early explorations and settlement in the 1968 edition of *Rise of the American Nation* mentions the contributions of the African American.

2. The 1982 edition of *Rise of the American Nation* admits in a chapter of the textbook that focuses on black Americans that blacks contributed to the early exploration and settlement of America.

3. Race relations are discussed on two pages of the 1968 edition of the general American history textbook *Rise of the American Nation,* but it is discussed under the subtopic, "Segregation of the Races."

4. The 1982 edition of *Rise of the American Nation* addresses race relations in the United State more generously. Eleven pages in the 1982 edition of *Rise of the American Nation* focus primarily on race relations in the United States. In addition, several   photographs of well-known blacks such as W.E.B. DuBois, Frederick Douglass, and Malcolm X who fought to improve race relations in America are mentioned in the 1982 edition.

5. The presence of African-American role models in the 1968 edition of *Rise* of the American Nation includes one line about Duke Ellington, jazz great, and four lines about Phillis Wheatley, one of the best known poets of colonial New England. Mary McLeod Bethune is also mentioned as one of the prominent leaders who made up President Franklin Roosevelt's "black cabinet." A. Phillip Randolph, President of the Brotherhood of sleeping Car Porters' Labor Union is recognized for the pressure he place on President Franklin Roosevelt in threatening to organize 10,000 Negroes to march on the national capital to demand equal employment opportunities. Roosevelt responded by establishing the Fair Employment Practices committee in June of 1941.

6. The 1982 edition of *Rise of the American Nation* includes several African-American role models such as Edward Johnson, textbook author; James Meredith, a 29-year-old air force veteran, who tried to enroll at the University of Mississippi; Sourjouner Truth, who is included in the 1982 edition of *Rise of the American Nation* as one of the leaders of the Women's Movement.

7. The 1968 edition of *Rise of the American Nation* appraises the black church in the context of the colonialization and condemnation of it by free blacks.

8. The 1982 edition of Rise of the American Nation appraises the black church in reference to the significance of the Anti-Slavery Movement and the Civil Rights Movement.

9. Civil Rights and the black American are mentioned on sixteen pages of the 1968 edition of the general American history textbook *Rise of the American Nation.* The discussion begins with slavery and continues through the Civil Rights Movement.

10. The 1982 edition of *Rise of the American Nation* goes into more detail about civil rights than the 1968 edition. The 1968 edition uses more denotative language in describing events such as the crisis in Little Rock, the Montgomery Bus Boycott, and Brown vs. Board of education of Topeka, Kansas. Its candid description of the information is based on fat rather than emotion as perhaps the 1968 edition represents.

11. The 1968 edition of *Rise of the American Nation* devotes a couple of paragraphs on two pages to the resistance of slavery.

12. The 1982 edition of *Rise of the American Nation* discusses, candidly, on five pages, the resistance to slavery.

13. The 1968 edition of *Rise of the American Nation* devotes fur pages to the education of black Americans.

14. The 1968 edition of *Rise of the American Nation* mentions two (2) black inventors: George Washington Carver and Elijah McCoy.

15. The contributions that blacks made to the building of America are not discussed, specifically, in the 1968 edition of *Rise of the American Nation*; however, blacks are mentioned throughout the textbook.

16. The 1982 edition of *Rise of the American Nation* mentions the contributions of groups of black America such as cowboys and congresspersons.

17. The discussion of black inventors in the 1968 edition of *Rise of the American Nation* mentions one black scientist/inventor George Washington Carver, under the subheading: "limited Progress of Negroes."

18. The 1968 edition of rise of the American Nation mentions two black inventors: George Washington Carver and Elijha McCoy.

19. The old South is discussed in the 1968 edition of *Rise of the American Nation* in the context of slavery, reconstruction, "Jim Crow" laws, civil rights and education.

20. The 1982 edition of *Rise of the American Nation* discusses the inhumane system slavery and the resistance of it by Americans such as Frederick Douglass, Harriet Tubman, Lloyd Garrison, Denmark Vesey and Nat Turner.

Summary

This comparison of two (2) general American history textbooks was done to analyze the differences in the African American presence. The 1968 edition and the 1982 edition of the American history textbook *Rise of the American Nation* were analyzed.

Many factors contributed to the distortions, limitations and misrepresentations of African Americans in American history textbooks prior to and including the 1968 edition of *Rise of the American Nation*.

The nation was in a state of unrest in 1968, and many influential personalities in society concluded that the African American was causing many of his or her problems by rioting and killing. These opinions of influential persons in society influenced what was printed about the African American in the 1968 edition of *Rise of the American Nation*

After the death of Dr. Martin Luther King, Jr., many African Americans and Whites felt that the Civil Rights Movement had ended, therefore, specific groups in society began pressuring American textbook publishers to place the African American in his proper perspective in American history textbooks.

As time passed, many influential personalities in society began changing their attitudes and beliefs about African Americans. These changes in attitudes and viewpoints were reflected in the 1982 edition of the American history textbook *Rise of the American Nation*.

The African American had been portrayed as one who had made limited contributions to society in the 1968 edition of *Rise of the*

American Nation. In the 1982 edition of *Rise of American Nation*, the African American was portrayed as a contributor to and participant in American history.

In the 1968 edition of *Rise of the American Nation,* the African American gave no views on domestic issues. In the 1982 edition of *Rise of the American Nation,* several Black views on domestic issues were included.

The 1968 edition of *Rise of the American Nation* included limited information about Black organizations, while the 1982 edition of *Rise of the American Nation* included detailed information about Black organizations.

The 1968 edition of *Rise of the American Nation* distorted facts about slavery and its impact on American society. The 1982 edition of *Rise of the American Nation* gave detailed information about slavery and its impact on American society.

The comparison of the presence of the African American in these two (2) general American history textbooks gave an idea of what changes were made in the African American's image in a span of fourteen (14) years.

Conclusions and Recommendations

Introduction

The purpose of this study was to analyze the differences in the African American's presence as portrayed in an earlier and later edition of a general American history textbook. The 1968 edition and the 1982 edition of *Rise of the American Nation* were analyzed, and the following information was obtained from this analysis.

There was a significant difference in the African American's presence in the 1968 edition and the 1982 edition of *Rise of the American Nation.* The 1968 edition of *Rise of the American Nation* had very little information about the African American and his or her contributions. The 1982 edition of *Rise of the American Nation* gave more information about the African American and his or her contributions to the building of America. The 1968 edition of *Rise of the American Nation* distorted facts about slavery and its impact on American life. The 1982 edition of *Rise of the American Nation* included more detailed information about slavery and its impact on this society. The 1968 edition of *Rise of the American Nation* gave no African American views on domestic issues. The 1982 edition of *Rise of the American Nation* gave African American views on domestic issues. The African American's image changed significantly in the 1982 edition of *Rise of the American Nation.*

Conclusions

The comparison of two (2) general American history textbooks was done to analyze the differences in the image of the African American. Based on the findings of this study, the following conclusions can be drawn:

(a) Many significant contributions of the African American were never placed in earlier American history textbooks.

(b) The African American was portrayed in a stereotyped image in earlier American history textbooks.

(c) The change in the African American's image in later published American history textbooks was due to changes in attitudes, opinions, research methods, communication with African Americans and accurate historical facts about African Americans and Americans in general.

(d) The changes in the African American presence in later published American history textbooks was due to pressure from certain groups in society.

(e) The limitations of some textbook publishers concerning the African American presence was due to the traditions and values of certain groups in society.

(f) The limitations of some textbook publishers concerning the African American presence were due to specific group interests.

(g) The limitations of some textbook publishers concerning the African American presence was due to certain beliefs of influential personalities in society.

(h) The limitations of some textbook publishers concerning the African American presence were due to the structure of the system.

(i) The limitations of some textbook publishers concerning the African American presence were due to domestic needs.

(j) Some later textbook publishers tried to put the African American in his proper perspective.

(k) The limitations of some textbook publishers concerning the African American presence were due to lack of communication with the African American.

(l) The changes in the African American presence in later published American history textbooks were due to more communication with African Americans.

® African-American students still complain that their high-school American history textbooks do not have sufficient information about activities and events related to African Americans in the development of American society.

(s) The 1968 edition of *Rise of the American Nation* mentions one black inventor, but the 1982 edition mentions two black inventors.

(t) The old South in the 1968 edition of *Rise of the American Nation* is discussed in the context of slavery, reconstruction, "Jim Crow" laws, civil rights and education.

(u) The 1982 edition of Rise of the American Nation in reference to the old South discusses the inhumane system of slavery, and the resistance of slavery by Americans such as Frederick Douglass, Harriet Tubman, Lloyd Garrison, and Sojourner Truth.

Recommendations

The African American presence changed significantly in American history textbooks during the fourteen (14) year span from 1968 to 1982. American history textbook publishers began including information that had not been included before about the African American and his contributions to American society. The 1982 edition of *Rise of the American Nation* portrayed the African American as a participant in and contributor to American history, instead of a stereotyped bystander who had no history. Based on the foregoing conclusions, it is recommended that:

(a) The contributions of the African American be included in all American history textbooks.

(b) The impact of slavery be included in all American history textbooks.

© The stereotyped images of slaves be excluded from American history textbooks.

(d) All students be helped to develop critical thinking, critical reading, and active learning skills consistent with a goal of making each student a life-long learner.

(e) The myths of the African American be replaced with the truth.

(f) African-American students be made aware of the fact that concerned. Whites stood ready to help the African American in his or her fight for equality.

(g) Teachers play a more significant role in the teaching of American history.

(h) Teachers take a few units from American history textbooks and state what should be emphasized about Blacks and their contributions.

(i) Teachers instill in African-American students a pride in their African-American heritage.

(j) American history textbook publishers consult African-American historians about American history.

Epilogue

Many issues will impact African Americans and their presence in American history textbooks in the new millennium: affirmative action, racial profiling, reverse discrimination, and hate crimes are several issues of concern. Also, the effect of information technology on minorities and effective programs used in teaching the "minority will be discussed. However, determining how effectively textbook publishers have dealt with these issues has not been documented.

According to Teresa Amot and Julie Matthaei in their book *Race Gender and Work* (1996), affirmative action programs are programs intended to better the positions of women and minorities in the workforce. They encompass a broad spectrum, including public policies such as set asides and contract compliance. Set asides force government organizations to purchase a certain percentage of their goods and services from minority or women owned companies. Contract compliance obligates companies that do business with governments to diversify their employee base. Affirmative action programs also include an array of voluntary efforts and policies made by privately owned businesses and educational institutions. These actions influence hiring or promotion efforts and admissions publicizing job openings or using a greater variety of qualifications for admission to broaden and diversify the workforce or student body policies. Steps taken toward affirmative action can be as simple as more widely. Lastly, affirmative action also includes legislation to prevent discrimination or attack it where it has been found.

Affirmative action has been a controversial subject, which has caused much tension in American society. However, the debate over affirmative action has become ensnared in rhetoric that pits equality of opportunity against the equality of results. The debate has been more emotional than intellectual, and has generated more tension than results.

Another issue that will impact the African-American presence in American history textbooks is the discriminatory practice by police of treating (blackness and brownness) as an indication of possible criminality—has lately been the focus of frequent legal legislative action resulting in a significant amount of coverage in mainstream media such as the **New York Times** and **Nightline** (Muharrar, Mikal 1).

Many believe that there is need for a broader understanding of "racial profiling." It may best be understood as the politically acceptable and very American practice of defining a social problem in "blackface." The "blackness" of the problem encourages suspicion, polarizing antagonism, and typically leads to the targeting of the racial group for punitive (public policy) action.

Examples of issued defined in blackface and subjected to a racial profile include the black drug abuser and drug dealer, the threatening and invasive black criminal, the black welfare cheat and queen, and the undeserving black affirmative action recipient. The punitive actions associated with drugs, crime, welfare and affirmative action policy is self-evident, and involves punitive action disproportionately affecting African-American people.

Given the prevalence of racial profiling documented here and elsewhere, it only makes sense that a recent survey of young people found that they not only recognized that racial stereotyping was rampant on television but that TV news was a worse perpetrator of racial stereotyping than TV's entertainment programming.

Across all races, children are more likely to associate positive characteristics with white characters and negative characteristics with minority characters. "A Different World: Children's Perceptions of Race and Class in the Media" reported that "children of all races agree that the news media tend to portray African-American and Latino people more negatively than white and Asian people, particularly when the news is about young people."

Another issue that will impact society and the African American presence in American history textbooks is reverse discrimination. With many lawsuits being file by White Americans who are alleging that Blacks are been promoted and or hired before they are, even though they are more qualified, the African American status in society and in American history textbooks is being threatened.

Recently, a fire department lieutenant was passed over (for the second time) in favor of an African-American man pursuant to the department's affirmative action plan. The percentage of African-American men in the department meets or exceeds EEOC recommendations. The passed-over firefighters are considering filing suit.

How reverse discriminations lawsuits will affect the African-American presence in American history has yet to be determined. But, if the truth were told, it would validate that reverse discrimination lawsuits should not affect the presence of African Americans in American history textbooks. However, the majority of textbook publishers are White, and one cannot adequately evaluate how reverse discrimination as a political issue will affect textbook publishers.

Hate crimes are prevalent in society today, and these crimes impact all Americans, but especially African Americans because they are among the least in society, along with gays and Asians.

Recently, a black man was dragged to his death behind a pick-up truck, and a gunman shot another black randomly. These kinds of crimes have outraged most of society, but Congress has yet to pass severe laws against hate crimes.

All in all, African Americans will continue to try and validate their worthiness of inclusion in American history. However, changes will occur slowly because African Americans and other minorities have not understood the urgency of being portrayed accurately and consistently in American history textbooks.

How affirmative action, racial profiling, reverse discrimination, and hate crimes will impact the presence of African Americans in American history textbook will be determined by the need of textbooks publishers to tell the historical truth regardless of how it will affect groups who have special interests in society.

Information technology is probably the fastest growing area of technology today. Advances in the microelectronics and such optical devices as fiber optics and lasers have been fundamental driving forces behind these changes. Such advances are expected to promote a continuing extension of innovation at all levels of the global economy. Telecommunications technology will likely be changing at the same rate, transmitting tens of millions of characters of information per second over a fiber optics telephone that these technological changes are merely the instruments of catalysts for sound, cultural and economic change. Information related jobs, according to Nilles, will expand to three-fifths of health in many direct ways. Computer-aided design helps automobile manufacturers to build cars that are structurally safer; conditions and prevent intoxicated drivers from driving. Health care begins at home. As more households get personal computers, health-care software will help improve families' diet and exercise patterns. As simple as this sounds, it can be a material factor in improving health conditions worldwide.

How information technology will affect the minority presence in American history textbooks has not been determined. However, the excitement of computer-assisted learning is that:

1.   Students are deeply engaged in a pro-and interactive mode of learning.

2. Teachers are resources and facilitators of learning in an environment characterized by psychological, sociological, and communal health.

3.   Teachers participate with their students in retrieving, interpreting, integrating, and sharing learning.

4. Teachers model trust, mutual respect, multicultural awareness and sensitivity, and a willingness to engage others with an appreciation of the uniqueness of the individual.

5. This proposal will enhance teaching and learning in freshmen English—English Literature and Composition I and II in the following ways:

6. Teachers will share their best wisdom, strategies, and philosophies—addressing the fundamental issues and concerns.

7. Faculty will be presented with a syllabus, which represents a student- centered learning paradigm.

As Atberry, Barr, and Tagg *(From Teaching to learning—A New Paradigm for Undergraduate Education 1995)* suggest, in a learning focused organization, the emphasis is on quality of learning process in a trustworthy and validating environment with a series of ongoing assessment of learning. Within this context, special emphasis will be place on:

1. The assessment of knowledge bases and information before the beginning of the course.

2. The assessment of knowledge bases and information at the midpoint of the course

3. The assessment of knowledge bases and information at the conclusion of the course.

4. Each class would use advanced computer technology within the parameters of the course to determine efficacy of computer-assisted learning, and the role of the teacher as supportive mentor, co-learner, and facilitator.

5. A simple evaluation from each student as to initial course expectations, learning style, and experience in the course with regard to learning process.

In conclusion, teaching and learning with technology will be the trend of the 21st century. Students and teachers will be using the computer as one of the tools to assist students in the learning process. As education shifts toward student-centered learning, the teachers will be asked to support this process as mentor, co-learner, and facilitator. Using technology in teaching and learning is not going to suddenly disappear. Therefore, educators, curricular committees, and principally textbook publishers must keep abreast of technology and its effects on all   students,   but   especially   minority   students.

Glossary

This glossary will assist a reader in understanding several of the terms used in this document. Additionally, it will ensure a reader's awareness of the context of these terms. Moreover, is a reader is reading this book and discovers a word that her or she does not understand he or she can turn to the glossary immediately and find the meaning of that word.

Abolitionist	One who advocated the abolishment of slavery.
African American	American of African descent.
Diversity	State of being varied; variety.
Diaspora	Any country that has descendants of Africa; a dispersion of an originally homogeneous people.
Distort	To give false significance to, to misrepresent.
Ghetto	Area of a town lived in by any minority national or social group typically crowded and with poor housing conditions.

Glossary

Hagiography	Literature dealing with the lives of saints. A collection of sacred writings.
Historigraphical	History of visual symbols, lettering, diagrams, drawings.
Inferiority	Situated under or beneath.
Image	The character projected by someone or something to the public.
Interracial	Between or involving different. Races.
Intergroup Attitudes	Attitudes between or involving different groups.
Interpersonal Behavior	Behavior existing or done between two people.
Middle Passage	The passage between Africa and America.
Minority	Small group in a community,

Glossary

	nation, etc., differing from others in race, religion, language, etc.
Multiculturalism	Of, relating or to, intended for several individual cultures.
Limitation	Condition, fact or circumstance that limits.
omission	The act of disregarding or neglecting to acknowledge.
Perspective	Subjective evaluation of relative significance; point of view.
Pivot	Central point, pin or shaft on which something turns.
Portray	To represent, to describe vividly in words.
Racial	Of, pertaining to, or typical of an ethnic group.

Glossary

Sambo   A stereotyped example of a dull
                                        witted, happy-go-lucky, banjo
                                        strumming slave.

Stereotyped   something conforming to a fixed or
                                        general pattern; a standardized
                                        mental picture held in common by
                                        members of a group representing
                                        an oversimplified opinion, or affective
                                        attitude, or uncritical judgment (as   of
                                        a person, race, an issue or
                                        event).

Bibliography

Adams, Barbara et al. "Writing for Learning: How to Achieve a Total College Commitment." April 1985, ED 258 666.

Ammon, Paul and Mary Sue Ammes. "Using Student Writing to Assess and Promote Understanding in Science." 1990, ED 3116864.

Andrews, William L., Ed. *African American Autobiography: A Collection of Critical Essays.* New Jersey: Prentice-Hall, Inc., 1993.

Ani, Marimba. *Yurugu: An Afrivan-Centered Critique of European Thought and Behavior.* Trenton: Arica World Press, 1992.

Asante, Molefi Kete. *Malcolm X as Cultural Hero and other Essays.* New Jersey: African World Press, Inc., 1993.

Awkward, Michael, Ed. New Essays on *Their Eyes Were Watching God.* Cambridge: Cambridge University Press, 1990.

Barber, Lucius J. *Our Time Has Come.* Chicago: University of Illinois Press, 1979.

Barndt, Joseph. *Dismantling Racism: The Continuing Challenge to White America.* Minneapolis: Augsburg Press, 1991.

Barzun, Jacques and Henry Graff. The Modern Researcher. New York: Harcourt Brace Javanovich, Inc., 1977.

Bibliography

Bell, Derrick. "Learning the Three T's of America's Slave Heritage." In
Slavery and the Law, Paul Finkleman, ed. Madison House, 1997.

Bennett, Lerone. *The Shaping of Black America.* Chicago: Johnson
Publishing   Company, Inc., 1993.

Berry Faith, Ed. *A Scholar's Conscience: Selected Writings of J.
Saunders Redding, 1942-1977.* Kentucky: The University Press of
Kentucky, 1992.

Berry, Mary Frances and John Blassingame. *Long Memory: The Black
Experience in America.* New York: Oxford University Press, 1982.

Bethel, Lorraine "'This Infinity of Conscious Pain': Zora Neale
Hurston and the BlackTradition." In Harold Bloom, "Modern
Interpretations of Zora Neale   Hurston's *Their Eyes Were
Watching God.*" New York: Chelsea House, 1987.

The Bible. King James Version. Michigan: World Publishing, 1989.

Blassingame, John W., Ed. The Frederick Douglass Papers. Series 1
Speeches, Debates, and Interviews, Vols. 1-4. New Haven: Yale
University Press, 1979.

Bloom, Alan. *The Closing of the American Mind, New York:* Simon and
Schuster, 1987.

Bloom, Harold, Ed. *Zora Neale Hurston.* New York: Chelsea House,
1986.

_____ Harold, Ed.   Modern Critical Interpretations: Zora Neale

Hurston's *Their Eyes   Were Watching God.*

Borman, K., Timm, P., Zakia, E., and Winston, M. 1992. "Using
   Multiple Strategies to Assess Multicultural Education in a School
   District." In Carl Grant (ed.). *Research and Multicultural
   Education.* Education: Washington: The Falmer Press.

Braxton, Joanne M. *Black Women Writing Autobiography: A Tradition
   Within A Tradition.* Philadelphia: Temple University Press, 1989.

Butler, J. 1993. "Transforming the Curriculum: Teaching about
   Women of Color." In J. Banks and C. Banks (eds.). Multicultural
   Education: Issues and Perspectives (2nd ed.). Boston: Allyn and
   Bacon.

Butler, Johnella E. and Schmitz, Betty. 1991. "Different Voices: A
   Model Institute for Integrating Women of Color into Undergraduate
   American Literature and History Courses."In J. C. Butler and J.C.
   Walter, (eds.) *Transforming the Curriculum: Ethnic Studies and
   Women's Studies.* Albany, NY: SUNY Press.

Campbell, Karlyn Kohrs. "Style and Content in the Rhetoric of early
   Afro- American Feminists." *Quarterly Journal of Speech* 72
   (1986: 441- 443.Christian, Barbara. *Black Feminist Criticism:
   Perspectives on Black Women Writers* NewYork: Pergamon Press,
   1986.

Cooke, Virginia. Writing Across the Curriculum: A Faculty Handbook.
   Victoria. Centre for Curriculum and Professional Development, 1991.

Cruse, Harold. *The Crisis of the Negro Intellectual: A Historical*

Bibliography

Analysis of the Failure of Black Leadership. New York: Quill, 1967.

_____. *1968 Rebellion Revolution.* In Maulana Karenga's Introduction
   to Black Studies. Los Angeles Sankore Press, 1989.

Dertouzos, Michael L. "Communications, Computers and Networks."
   Scientific American Sept. 1991; 2-69.

Douglass, Frederick. *My Bondage and my Freedom.* New York: The
   Freedman's Press, 1855.

_____. *Narrative of the Life of Frederick Douglass.* New York:
   Freedmen's Press, 1848.

Du Bois, W.E.B. *Dusk of Dawn: An Essay Toward and Autobiography of
   a Race Concept.* New Brunswick: Transaction Publishers, 1991.

Dyson, Michael Eric. *Reflecting Black: African American Cultural
   Criticism.* Minneapolis University of Minnesota Press, 1993.

Epperson, D.C. "Making Social Critics of Disadvantaged Children."
   Social Education 35 (1968): 52.

Franklin, John Hope. *From Slavery to Freedom.* New York: Alfred
   A.Knopf, Inc., 1947.

Fuller, Chet. *I Hear them Calling my Name: A Journey Through the New
   South.* Boston: Houghton Mifflin Company, 1989.

Gerf, Vinton. "Networks." *Scientific American* Sept. 1991: 72-81.

Bibliography

Gill, Walter. *Issues in African American Education*. Nashville: Winston-Derek Publishers, 1991.

Harlan, L.R. "Tell it like it was: Suggestions on Black History." *Social Education* 30 (1969): 405.

Harrison, C.H. "Black History and the Schools." *Ebony* Dec. 1968: 111.

Hatch, Roger M. et al., Eds. *Reverend Jesse L. Jackson: Straight from the Heart*. Philadelphia: Fortress Press, 1987.

Henry, Charles P. *Jackson: The Search for Common Ground*. Chelsea House Publishers, 1988.

Hemenway, Robert. "The Personal Dimension in Their Eyes Were Watching god." In Michael Awkward, New Essays on Their Eyes Were Watching God. Cambridge: Cambridge University Press, 1990.

Hicks, John. "Discovery." In N.Y. Nathiri, *Zora! Zora Neal Hurston: A Woman and Her Community*. Orlanda: Sentinel Communications Company, 1991.

Holloway, Karla. *The Character of the Word: The Texts of Zora Neal Hurston*. Chicago: University of Illinois Press, 1987.

Holsti, K.J. *International Politics: A Framework for Analysis*. New Jersey: Prentice Hall, Inc., 1972.

Holt, Elvin. Fifty Southern Writers After 1900. Westport Conn: Greenwood Press, 1987.

Hook, Bell and Cornel West. *Breaking Bread. Insurgent Black*

Bibliography

Intellectual Life. Boston: South End Press, 1991.

Huggins, Nathan Irvin. *Black Americans of Achievement.* New York:
Chelsea House Publishers, 1988.

Hurston, Zora Neale. *Their Eyes Were Watching God.* Read by Ruby
Dee. Audiocassette. Harper, ISBN111-55941, 1991.

_____, Zora Neale. *Their Eyes Were Watching God. Publishers
Weekly.* 6 Dec. 1991: 44.

_____. Zora Neale. *Dust Track on a Road.* Philadelphia: J. B.
Lippincott, 1937.

Jacobs, William Jay. *Great Lives.* New York: Charles Scribner's Sons,
1990.

Johnson, E.A. *A School History of the Negro Race in America.* New
York: Goldman   Co., 1911.

Johnson, Michael P. and James L. Roark. *Black Masters: A Free Family
of Color in the Old   South.* New York: W.W. Norton and Company,
1984.

Joyce, W. "Afro-American Studies: A Policy Analysis." *Viewpoints*
51 (1975) : 45-46.

Karenga, Maulana. *Introduction to Black Studies.* Los Angeles:
University of Sankore Press, 1989.

Bibliography

Katz, W.L. *Teacher's Guide to American Negro History*. Chicago:
Quadrangle Books, 1968.

Kerlinger, Fred N. *Foundations of Behavioral Research*. New York:
Holt, Rinehart and Winston, Inc., 1966.

King, Colbert I. "What Would Dr. King Think." *Washington Post* 13
January 1996: A19.

King, Coretta Scott. "From Marion, Ala., to the Mountaintop of the
Dream." *Ebony* November 1995: 56.

King, Martin Luther, Jr. *Stride Toward Freedom*. San Francisco:
Harper and Row Publishers, 1958.

Kubitschek, Missy Dehn. "Tu de Horizon and Back': The Female
Quest in *Their Eyes Were Watching God*." In Harold Bloom,
"Modern Critical Interpretations of Zora Neale Hurston's Their
Eyes Were Watching God." New York: Chelsa House, 1987.

Lambropoulos, Vassilis. *The Rise of Euro centrism: Anatomy of*
Interpretation. New Jersey: The Princeton University Press, 1993.

Landers, Thomas H. and Richard M. Quinn. *Jesse Jackson and the*
Politics of Race. Ottwa: First Impressions, Inc., 1985.

Lemonick, Michael D. "Tomorrow's Lesson: Learn or Perish." *Time*
Oct. 1992: 59.

Lewis, Earl. "Writing Afro cam Americans into a History of
Overlapping   Diasporas." *American Historical* Review. (1995)
765- 787.

Bibliography

Lincoln, C. Eric. (1974) *The Black Church Since Frazier*. In Maulana
    Karenga's Introduction *to Black Studies*. Los Angeles: University
    of Sankore Press, 1989.

Litwack, Leon F. *Been in the Storm so Long: The Aftermath of Slavery.*
    New York: Alfred Knoff, 1979.

Logan, Shirley. "Rhetorical Strategies in Ida B. Wells ' 'Southern
    Horrors: Lynch Law in all   its Phases. Sage. Vol. VIII, No. 1
    (Summer 1991).

Long, R.A. "Black Studies Fall into Place." Nation 219 (1974): 19-20.

Lonsway, F. A. "Cultural and Social Natures in the School Organization."
    Clearing House 40 (1966) 387-390.

Loury, Glenn C. "The Public Interest." In   William Raspberry's *Looking
    Backward at Us*. Jackson: Jackson University Press of Mississippi,
    1991.

Lupton, Mary Jane. "Black Women and Survival in *Comedy American
    Style* and Their Eyes *Were Watching God*." Zora Neale Hurston
    Forum 1, no. 1 (fall 1986): 38-44.

Madaras, H. and Matlick, M. 1993. "Impact of Specified Course
    Completion on the Awareness of Cultural Diversity." On the MARC.
    3(1): 14 College Park MD: Maryland Assessment Resource Center.

Marable, Manning. *Beyond Black and White: Transforming African-
    American Politics*. New York: Verso, 1995.

Marimba, Ani. Yurugu: *An African Centered Critique of European
    Thought, Culture,*

Bibliography

and Behavior. Trenton, New Jersey: Africa World Press, 1994.

Martin, Waldo E., Jr., *The Mind of Frederick Douglass.* Chapel Hill: The University of North Carolina Press, 1985.

Matney, William C., Ed. *Who's Who Among Black Americans.* 5th Ed. Lake Forest, IL: Educational Communications, 1988.

Meese, Elizabeth A. *Crossing the Double Cross: The Practice of Feminist Criticism.* Chapel Hill: University of North Carolina Press, 1986.

Meier, August. "Benjamin Quarles and the Historiography of Black America." *Civil War History* 26 (1980 101-106.

Metzger, Linda and A. Straub Ed. *Contemporary Authors: Bio-Bibliographical Guide to Current Writers in Fiction, General Nonfiction, Poetry, Journalism, Drama, Motion Pictures, Television and Other Fields.*Vol. 16 Detroit: Gale Research, 1986.

Newson, Adele S. *Zora Neale Hurston: A Reference Guide.* Boston: G.K. Hall, 1987.

Paludi, M. and Tronto J. 1992. "CUNNY-Hunter College Feminist Education." In Caryn M. Musil (ed.) The *Courage to Question: Women's Studies and Student Learning.* Washington, DC: Association of American Colleges.

Pertiz, Janice H. "When Learning is Not Enough: Writing Across the

Bibliography

Curriculum and the (RE) turn to Rhetoric." Internet JAC 14.2, fall
1994.

Pondrom, Cyrena N. "The Role of Myth in Hurston's *Their Eyes Were
Watching God.*" American Literature 58 (May 1986): 181-202.

Proctor, Samuel D. "Black Contributions to the American Experience.
"National Elementary Principal 49 (1969): 19-22.

Quarles, Benjamin. "The Antebellum Free Negro*." Baltimore Bulletin
of Education* 45   (1969): 12-15.

_____. "Breach Between Douglass and Garrison." *Journal of Negro
History 25* (1938): 144-54.

_____. "Frederick Douglass and the Women's Rights Movement."
Journal of Negro History 25 (1940): 35-44. *Frederick Douglass.*
Washington: Associated Press, 1948.

_____. *The Negro in the Civil War.* Boston: Little, Brown, 1953.

_____. *Black Abolitionist.* New York: Oxford University Press,
1969.

_____. "Black History Unbound". *Daedalus* 103 (1974): 163-178.

Bibliography

_____. "Black History's Diversified Clientele." In *Black Mosaic: Essays in Afro-American History and Historiography*. Amherst: University of Massachusetts, 1988.

Ransome, Cora Upshur. "Results of Sponsored Writing Center Program to Eliminate Students' Deficiencies in Preparation to Retake the English Proficiency Examination." Bowie State University, 1994.

Raspberry, William. *Looking Backward at Us*. Jackson: University Press of Mississippi, 1991.

Reynolds, Barbara A. *Jesse Jackson: America's David*. Washington: JFK Associates, 1985.

Richards, Judith J. 1993. "Classroom Tapestry." In Theresa Perry and James Frases (eds.) *Freedom's Plow*. NY: Routledge.

Rist, Ray C. *The Invisible Children: School Integration in American Society*. Massachusetts: Harvard University Press, 1978.

Rose, Willie Lee. *Slavery and Freedom*. New York: Oxford University Press, 1982.

Rowan Carl T. *Just Between Us Blacks*. New York: Random House, 1974.

Schofield, Janet Ward. *Black and White in School: Trust, Tension, or Tolerance*. New York: Teachers College Press, 1989.

Bibliography

Shwartz, Robert A. Rev. of *Molding the Good Citizen: The Politics of High School History Texts* by Robert Lerner et al. *Teachers College ecord* 97 (1996): 664-66.

Scriven, Michael. *Evaluation Thesaurus*. (4th ed.). Newbury Park, CA: Sage Publications, 1991.

Sloan, I.J. *The American Negro: A Chronology and Fact Book*. New York: Oceana   Publications, Inc., 1968.

Stampp, K.M. *The Peculiar Institution*. New York: Vintage Books, 1956.

Sterling, D. *Lift Every Voice*. Garden City: Doubleday and Company, Inc., 1965.

Stewart, James B. (1979) "Introducing Black Studies: A Critical Examination of Some Textual Materials." In Maulana Karenga's *Introduction to Black Studies*. Los Angeles.   University of Sankore Press, 1989.

Sully, Brenda. "Malaspina University-College's Writing-Across-the-Curriculum Project 18 April 2000. htttp://www.mala.bc.ca/www/wac/proj.htm.

Sundquist, Eric J., Ed. *Frederick Douglass: New Literary and Historical* Essays. Cambridge: Cambridge University Press, 1990.

Tabb, William K. (1970). *The Political Economy of the Black Ghetto*. In   Maulana Karenga's Introduction *to Black Studies*. Los Angeles: University of Sankore Press, 1989.

Bibliography

Tetreault, Mary Kay Thompson. 1993. "Classrooms for Diversity: Rethinking Curriculum and Pedagogy." In J. Banks and C. Banks (eds.).

Multicultural Education: Issues and Perspectives (32nd ed.). Boston: Allyn and Bacon.

Todd, P.T. and M. Curti. *Rise of the American Nation*. New York: Harcourt, Brace and World, Inc., 1968.

Todd, P.T. and M. Curti. *Rise of the American Nation*. New York: Harcourt, Brace and Javonavich, 1982.

Van Deburg, William L. *Slavery and Race in American Popular Culture*. Wisconsin: University of Wisconsin Press, 1984.

Walton, Sidney F. (1974) "Towards a Critique of Social Science." In Maulana Karenga's Introduction *to Black Studies*. Los Angeles: University of Sankore Press, 1989.

Walvoord, Barbara E., MacCarthy, Lucille P. *Thinking and Writing in College: A Naturalistic St;udy of Students in Four Disciplines*. National Council of Teachers of English, Urgana, Illinois. Eric Ed 324591.

West, Cornel. *Keeping the Faith: Philosophy and Race in America*. New York Routledge, 1993.

Bibliography

Ibid. *Beyond Eurocentrism and Multiculturalism.* Maine: Common
Courage Press, 1993.

Weiser, Michael S. "Building on Common Ground: Overcoming.

Wesley, Charles H. *The Quest for Equality: From Civil War to Civil
Rights.* Pennsylvania: The Publishers Agency, Inc., 1978.

White, Edward M. "Shallow Roots or Taproots for Writing Across the
Curriculum." ADEBulliten. Spring. 1991, 29-33.

Whitney, Bob. "New Developments in the Teaching of Writing: A
Workshop." Inquiry: Critical Thinking Across the Disciplines.
Sept./Oct. 1993, 32-36.

Whitworth College. *Writing across the Curriculum.* Spokane:
Consortium   for the   Advancement of Private Higher Education,
1992.

Wilson, Julius William. *The Declining Significance of Race: Blacks and
Changing American   Institutions.* Chicago: Chicago University Press,
1978.

Writing Across the Curriculum (WAC) Proposal. 18 April 2000.
*h*ttp:www.marshall.edu/academic-affairs/MU_Info/mpwac.htm.>

Bibliography

Yancey, Kathleen Blake. *Looking Back as We Look forward: Historicizing Writing Assessment. CCC 50.3 (1999): 483-501.*

Young, Art and Toby Fulwiler. *Writing Across the Disciplines: Research Into Practice*. Portsmouth: Boynton/Cook Publishers, 1986.

Zinn, Howard. *A People's History of the United States*. New York: Harper and Row, 1980.

About the Author

Born in Northampton County on the Eastern Shore of Virginia, Dr. Cora Upshur-Ransome presently resides with her husband Mack in Temple Hills, Maryland. Currently, she is a Professor of English at Bowie State University in Bowie, Maryland.